Beyond Flour 2

A Fresh Approach to Gluten-Free Cooking & Baking

Enjoy!

Marie Porter

Photography by
Michael Porter

Celebration Generation

www.celebrationgeneration.com

Beyond Flour

First Edition, November 2016

I.S.B.N. 978-0-9976608-2-1

Published and Distributed by

Celebration Generation, LLC
P.O. Box 22315
Robbinsdale, MN 55422

www.celebrationgeneration.com

Cover Photos, Clockwise from Top left:

Pelmeni, page 92
Samosa, page 56
Pumpkin Pie with Maple Cream, page 156
Boneless Chicken Wings, page 116
Spiced Oatmeal Raisin Cookies, page 126

Acknowledgments

To kick things off in this little love fest, big thanks to my husband, Michael Porter.

As always, he's not only contributed a lot of hard work to this book itself - by doing the photography for it - but also a lot of support that goes unseen. Testing the recipes with me, doing mountain after mountain of dirty dishes while I'm in recipe development, and just generally putting up with me through the grueling task of developing and publishing a cookbook.

I married well!

As with the first Beyond Flour, this book was the result of a very successful Kickstarter campaign. It would not have happened without the help of the many backers, who not only contributed financial support, but also promotional help and feedback on development.

Big thanks go to those who supported the campaign for Beyond Flour 2, as well as the original 602 people who supported the first Beyond Flour. Without that initial support, we wouldn't be here again, with a sequel! Special thanks go out in particular to Lindy Visaya.

Table of Contents

Foreword

Gluten. Augh!

It's now several years into my auto-immune related problems with the stuff, and I still find the whole thing mind boggling. Gluten and I were best buddies! We accomplished SO much together, before my body decided to declare war on the stuff.

Those first couple of years were tough, convinced that I'd lost everything that was worth eating. I used those "all purpose" gluten-free flours, turning up results that were just barely edible... at best! Things didn't taste right, and tended to be either crumbly or gummy. Weird flavours and textures everywhere.

The thing is, I've been a problem solver my whole life. I've never been big on "This is the way things are, and you're just going to have to deal with it"... and that went double for the idea of being stuck with food that was only barely edible.

How handy it was, that the most useful aspects of my particular manifestation of Aspergers were all centered around over-developed senses! As I mentioned in Beyond Flour:

"I'm an Aspie. That is, I am firmly planted in the "Aspergers" section of the autism spectrum. Some call it a disorder, I like to think of it as my superpower... especially in the kitchen. Having ridiculously overdeveloped senses may be annoying at times (bright lights, loud noises)... but it's a huge plus when it comes to cooking. I can tell when the peaches at the grocery store are perfectly ripe, all the way from the deli section. I can replicate pretty much any dish, just from taste and appearance. I can smell when baked goods are ready to come out of the oven.

I bake like I cook, and vice versa. I'd never really seen a difference between cooking and baking, and it's only been recently that I've been exposed to this idea that people are either cooks, or bakers. To me, all cooking and baking is just chemistry and math... balance and proportion. You need a good balance of flavours, body, acid, etc in cooking, you need a balance of structure, leavening, etc in baking. I've always approached it all in the same way I've approached logic problems - in my head.

'If Jenny is twice the age of Bob, who's three years older than Sue...' Really isn't that far off from 'I want to make a pizza crust, cannot have gluten in it... but I want THESE properties', in my mind. Baking gluten free recipes from normal recipes by only swapping out the flour is akin to trying to solve the age problem by plugging in the ages of Jennys, Bobs, and Sues that you know in your life.

The thing is, flour is only one ingredient. Recipes aren't about one ingredient, they're about how multiple ingredients AND techniques work together to create a whole. To merely swap out the flour for a set of alternate flours is to ignore all of the ways supporting ingredients - and techniques - can be utilized to create something that you actually want to eat, rather than a mediocre facsimile of what you REALLY want."

As with the original Beyond Flour, the recipes in this book were all developed from scratch, rather than simply swapping flour out. Flours and ratios were carefully chosen to work the best for each individual recipe - both in flavour and texture. Liquid ratios were developed specific to each mixture of flours, to work best with the solubility / liquid retention of each mix, as it relates to the recipe.

In some cases, the techniques may vary from how a recipe is traditionally made... to coax out the best performance from the ingredients used.

When I developed the first Beyond Flour, I made the decision to test the recipes exclusively on people who were NOT gluten-free. I felt that this would result in the most accurate feedback, and it turned out to be a great idea! No offense intended to my fellow gluten-frees... but you have to admit that sometimes our desperation and sense of loss can... cloud our judgement!

As such, I kept that policy in place for this book, and I think you'll love the results - as with the original, the recipes in this book are excellent on their own, without the need for a qualifying compliments with "... for a gluten-free recipe"!

It's been a little weird to develop a cookbook as a sequel, rather than a standalone, one-of book on a unique subject. On one hand, I want this book to very much be an extension of the first. On the other, I'd like people to be able to pick this book up and know what's what, without having to read the first one.

As such, the first chapter - "Let's Get it Started" - remains largely unchanged from the original. The flours I use in this book are more or less the same from the original - they work the best, taste the best, and are the most readily available. While there are some new products coming out, or on the radar for the future, I'm a big fan of stability and accessibility. As such, I stayed with "tried and true", for the most part.

Enjoy!

- *Marie Porter*

Let's Get it Started

While I've mentioned that successful gluten-free cooking/baking isn't just about substituting the flours... having a good working knowledge of what flours are available, and how to use them is always a good thing.

Every gluten-free flour out there has unique characteristics - protein content, flavour, elasticity, structure, absorption. In my opinion, attempting to combine to just duplicate regular, all purpose flour would do disservice to your final dish.

While all purpose wheat flour is a good, easy catch-all, there are many things that alternate flours do better. When used properly, some will bake up with a crispier texture. Many taste better than regular flour, and most alternate flours are actually more nutritious than wheat flour.

As with all cooking, it's all about balancing flavours and other properties, as well as proportion. Before you can get to developing your own recipes for gluten-free cooking, it's good to know what those properties are. Here is a bit of an overview:

Name	Type	Notes
Amaranth	Flour	Dense flour with a unique, nutty flavour. Great for savoury breads
Arrowroot	Starch	Commonly used for thickening, like corn starch.
Brown Rice	Flour	Earthy flavour, can be used in place of white rice flour for most uses - it's more nutritious.
Buckwheat	Flour	This is one of the best flours to use in gluten free baking, as it has a neutral taste, and some of the same properties as regular flour - for that reason, many people will skip the use of gums when baking with it. High fibre. I prefer to use "light" or "white" buckwheat, rather than the dark default.
Cassava	Flour	Fairly new to the scene, but often gets confused with tapioca starch, which can be mislabeled as cassava flour. Cassava flour and tapioca starch come from the same plant, but by different processes. Actual cassava flour can be hard to find in local stores.
Coconut	Flour	Sweet, high in fibre.. But soaks up a ton of liquid from your dish. Essential for insanely delicious baked goods, in my opinion!
Corn	Flour	Exactly what it sounds like - flour made from corn! Finely ground, commonly used in Mexican cooking - such as for tamales. (Masa flour)
	Meal	Grittier than corn flour. Great for corn muffins, some crusts, etc
	Starch	Primarily used as a thickener, and a starch in baking.
Fava Bean	Flour	High protein flour, with a less aggressive taste than garbanzo bean flour

Garbanzo	Flour	High protein flour, with a slightly bitter taste. Can taste strongly of beans to some people - it's excellent in batters for deep frying. (Chickpea flour)
Garfava	Flour	Combination of Fava bean and Garbanzo bean flours. High protein, mild flavour. Best for savoury recipes.
Millet	Flour	One of my favourite flours to work with. Slightly sweet, great for baking with, good nutrition.
Nut , various	Flour	Almost any kind of nut you can imagine is also available as a flour... and you can usually make them at home, also. The "flours" tend to be more "meal" than flour texture, but are great for many uses, especially in cookies. They do add fats to the mix, so keep that in mind when substituting.
Oat	Flour	Heart healthy, much more nutritious than wheat flour. Great tasting - be sure to use certified gluten-free oat flour, to avoid cross contamination.
Potato	Flour	Used primarily in baking and batters. Can help hold moisture in a recipe.
	Starch	Used as a thickener, can substitute for corn starch for those sensitive to corn
Quinoa	Flour	High in protein, but should be used fairly sparingly - has a strong taste and can make recipes turn out crumbly if used too generously.
Sorghum	Flour	A sweet tasting flour, great to bake with - it behaves closest to wheat flour, of all the alternative flours. Sorghum is also commonly used in gluten-free brewing.
Soy	Flour	AKA kinako (when roasted) flour. Soy is a really common allergen - so I avoid using this one, myself. High protein, dense flour.
Sweet Rice	Flour	Typically found in Asian grocery stores, can also be called "glutenous rice flour" - but don't worry, it does NOT contain gluten. Sweet, and can be used SPARINGLY to add moisture to a dish. (Too much, and it will turn out gummy!)
Tapioca	Starch	Typically used as a thickener (can substitute for corn starch), and to add elasticity and/or a chewy texture to baked goods. Use sparingly - can give a gummy texture.
Teff	Flour	By far, Teff is best known for its use in Injera - a stretchy African bread. It's great for adding a bit of elasticity to a recipe. As with most gluten-free flours, it definitely works best in conjunction with other flours. (It lacks the strength to hold up most baked good recipes, etc)
White Rice	Flour	A really common flour in gluten-free cooking, but it definitely needs supporting ingredients - it doesn't hold together well on its own, leading to crumbly consistencies. White rice flour is a great addition to deep fried batters, as it can produce a crispier texture.
Wild Rice	Flour	Should be used sparingly, as it has a very aggressive taste. (Earthy, almost gamey!) Can be used as a thickener, or to add flavour to savoury baked goods and other dishes.

It would be unreasonable to expect anyone to acquire - and keep fresh! - every variety of gluten-free flour out there. For the purposes of this book, I kept the working flours limited to:

Amaranth Flour
Brown Rice Flour
Buckwheat Flour (white/light!)
Coconut Flour
Corn flour, Meal, and Starch
Garbanzo flour
Millet Flour
Oat Flour
Potato Flour
Potato Starch
Sorghum Flour
Sweet Rice Flour
Tapioca Starch
White Rice Flour

... yes, that still looks like a lot, I know - but it's worth it, I promise!

I recommend looking through the recipes, picking a few you're interested in, and seeing what flours are called for across them. As an example, I pretty much only use garbanzo flour for deep fried items, and tend to only use coconut flour for baked goods.

From there, I'd vote for going online and placing an order for a small bag - about 1 lb - of each of the flours you see yourself using. Get some nice canisters to keep them in - I bought tall glass ones at IKEA - and clearly label them.

After the first order of flours, you'll be able to develop a good idea of what you go through fastest, and what you should buy in bigger quantities. As an example, I always buy the sorghum and white buckwheat flours in 5lb bags, but I go through coconut flour fairly slowly - most recipes only call for 1/4 cup!

Anyway...

Beyond knowing what the flours taste like, and what they're good for... Tweaking your recipe techniques go a long way to increasing your success in gluten-free cooking and baking. Here are a few things to keep in mind, as you work through this book:

Absorption: The various alternate flours absorb liquid at different rates. Experiment with this, and learn to use it to your advantage. As an example, coconut flour sucks moisture out of a recipe far more than most other flours. Thus, it requires more liquid than many of the other flours do.

Additionally, absorption can affect the way you should handle certain flours. You know how you should soak dried beans in water overnight, before working with them? Well, that same thing applies to bean flours, also - generally speaking, you'll want to mix them into the liquid and let it stand for 10 minutes or so to soften, before proceeding with the recipe. It softens the flour, and makes a big difference to the texture of the final product!

Humidity can also be a concern with gluten-free baking. The alternative flours can be far more finicky than wheat flour, when it comes to liquids and humidity. If you live in a humid area/house.. You may want to decrease the moisture content in your recipe, if even just slightly. Experiment!

Expectations: Non-gluten flours behave differently than regular gluten flour. Even when a dish is going to turn out to be a VERY close match for the original, full-gluten version... it may not act like it, up til that point. That's ok!

Most bread doughs will be more like cake batter, than something you'd knead by hand. The base recipe I batter and deep fry foods is VERY thick, kind of goopy, and not quite as easy to dip in, as regular flour. It's all good - and it'll work out well in the end. Just don't expect it to work up in exactly the same way as you're used to!

Fermentation: While some gluten-sensitive people have no problems with gluten that has been fermented - soy sauce, beer, even some sourdough bread! - I recommend using gluten free beers and soy sauces whenever possible, ESPECIALLY if it's a matter of being Celiac. (VS autoimmune sensitivity, etc).

Moisture: One main problem with gluten-free baking is that things can turn out to be dry and/or crumbly if you're not careful. Adding a ton of liquid to a recipe isn't always the best idea, as it will reduce the structural integrity. So, it's good to be sneaky about it.

For some recipes, you can use moist, non-liquid ingredients to boost and hold the moisture in a dish. Think pureed fruit like applesauce, extra eggs, dried fruit, honey, yogurt, and/or sour cream. These items can be used to add great flavour and texture to the final dish, in addition to being a moisture solution.

Oats: Oats are a sticky issue for some. The Canadian Celiac Association has declared oats to be safe for consumption, so long as they're uncontaminated. I've never had a reaction, myself... and I love using oats and oat flours in my gluten-free baking. They taste great - much better than wheat flour - and they're heart healthy! However, just be sure that when you're using oats, that you're using oats that are certified gluten-free, just to be safe!

Structure:	The main property of wheat flour that can be lacking in alternate flours is the strength to hold up to certain types of baking - cakes, breads, etc.
	When it comes to breads, and bread like baking, you'll want to make sure to have a decent amount of protein in the recipe (whether from the alternate flours, eggs, or a combination thereof), as well as an ingredient(s) that act as a binder or glue. This can come from gums - commonly either xanthan or guar - and/or use of a sticky starch, such as tapioca starch.
	When it comes to cakes, quick breads, etc ... I like to use eggs for both protein supplementation and structure. Separating the eggs and whipping the whites to a stiff peak before folding into your cake batter goes a long way to providing the structure a cake needs to rise and *stand*. It's a bit more work - and dishes! - than the usual of just tossing whole eggs into the batter, but it makes a ton of difference to the final product.

One of the major complaints about gluten-free cooking is having to use "many" flours, and the expense involved with getting set up. I've found it's really best to look at them as individual ingredients, rather than a whole bunch of substitutions for one ingredient. Think of it like having a well stocked spice cabinet. Sure, the up-front expense stings a bit.. But upkeep isn't that bad, refilling as you need. Also, a well stocked spice rack makes cooking a LOT more fun - and tasty - than only having salt and pepper on hand!

A Note on Measuring

The way you measure your flours can impact the amount of flour that you get in any given measurement. Some people scoop, others spoon. Some level off with a flat edge, others shake off the excess. Some believe that how you measure will GREATLY impact how your recipe turns out, I happen to think that if you use the same technique for all of it, it'll come out fine - no need to stress.

If you're interested, these recipes were all developed by using the measuring cup to scoop the flour, tapping it off the side of the container to shake off excess / level what's in there.

A Note on Equipment

Generally speaking, these recipes will just require basic cooking equipment - bowls, measuring spoons/cups, pots, pans, and basic bakeware. A few require a specialty piece: Cannoli tubes, for instance. I've done my best to only include specialty equipment when it's something you'll probably get a lot of use out of, or are super cheap.

The one big exception? A lot of these recipes mention using a food processor. If there is one piece of equipment that will make your life easier in the kitchen, it is a food processor. Even if you pick up a secondhand one for next to nothing, I HIGHLY recommend it. Trust me on this.

If you don't have a food processor, there are other ways to achieve the same sort of thing.

For instances where a food processor is being used to make dough, you can mix it by hand, use a stand mixer, or use an electric hand mixer.

For instances where a food processor is being used to chop something, you can chop it by hand.

For instances where a food processor is being used to puree something, you can use a blender. When there is not a lot of liquid involved, you'll want to do it in very small batches, however.

Let's get to the recipes ...

Breakfast & Brunch

Lembas

This description is going to be long, because I want you to understand the kind of complete geekery that went into the development of this recipe. We were just a few short days from a trip to LA a party in celebration of "The Hobbit" - TheOneRing.Net's "One Last Party", and I decided that it was finally time to develop my own Lembas recipe. In my mind, it would be fun, and thematic to bring along on our little journey, as well as being healthier and cheaper than airport food. The facts are these…

Lembas is a type of Elvish bread / cake / biscuit from Tolkien's writings. First made by Yavanna from a special Elvish corn, it was nutritious, and known to be ridiculously sustaining – that "One small bite will fill the stomach of a grown man", etc. It's generally theorized that Lembas was based on hard tack – a very dry and bland bread product used for military rations and some traditional Newfoundland cooking.

"Eat little at a time, and only at need. For these things are given to serve you when all else fails. The cakes will keep sweet for many many days, if they are unbroken and left in their leaf-wrappings, as we have brought them. One will keep a traveler on his feet for a day of long labour, even if he be one of the tall men of Minas Tirith." – Fellowship of the Rings

"The food was mostly in the form of very thin cakes, made of meal that was baked a light brown on the outside, and inside was the colour of cream." – Fellowship of the Ring

In the movies, Lembas was shown to be a crumbly white biscuit type food. Apparently they used an unsweetened shortbread that tasted awful. They were presented wrapped in leaves, and tied up with twine. Tolkien has said that they contain honey, and the "fruit of the Mallorn tree", which was described as "Its fruit was a nut with a silver shale" in Unfinished Tales. So.. lots of random information to work with, in addition to my own assumptions… and nutritional goals for the finished product.

To me, I pictured this as a sweet thing, but not a DESSERT thing. They straight up mention its sweetness, after all. I pictured some of the sweetness coming from the (canon!) honey, but also from dried fruit, which would contribute to the nutrition of it. I figured that dried apples would work best, given the colour description of the interior, but that apricots were more in line with the complexity of flavour I was envisioning of Elven cuisine. I decided that there should be a small amount of spice for complexity, and a pinch of herbs to bring it back from being too desserty. In terms of "fruit of the Mallorn tree", I chose to interpret that as almonds.

Now, in terms of the nutritious / sustenance properties of Lembas… I wouldn't have used white flour even if we weren't working around gluten issues. There's just no real nutrition there. I decided to use a small amount of masa flour, due to the original Lembas being corn based.

Because I have no elven magical corn, it'll have to do! Also, I'm supplementing it with protein powder and ground flax to contribute to nutrition. Non-magical, non-Valar corn is only slightly more nutritious than wheat flour, after all.

These are fantastic, and are VERY true to description: I personally can't eat a whole one at a time, as they are VERY filling. Note: If you are sensitive to oat flour, feel free to substitute millet flour.

Makes about 8 large biscuits

Butter, softened	1 cup	250 ml
Honey	1/3 cup	75 ml
Milk	2 Tbsp	30 ml
Masa flour	½ cup	125 ml
Gluten-free oat flour	½ cup	125 ml
Vanilla protein powder*	½ cup	125 ml
Sliced almonds	½ cup	125 ml
Thinly sliced dried apricots	½ cup	125 ml
Coconut flour	1/4 cup	50 ml
Ground flax seed (flax meal)	1/4 cup	50 ml
Tapioca starch	1 Tbsp	15 ml
Baking powder	1 tsp	5 ml
Xanthan gum	1 tsp	5 ml
Salt	½ tsp	2 ml
Ground cardamom	3/4 tsp	3 ml
Rosemary, finely chopped	1/4 tsp	1 ml
Corn starch, for rolling		

Mix butter and honey together just until combined – do not cream it or over beat it. Add milk, gently mix until combined and smooth.

In a separate bowl, whisk together remaining ingredients. Add dry mix to butter and honey, mix until combined. Wrap dough in plastic film, chill for 1 hour.

Preheat the oven to 350 F (180 C), line baking sheets with parchment paper.

Generously sprinkle clean work surface with corn starch, roll dough to ½" thick. Cut into 3" squares, and carefully transfer biscuits to prepared baking sheets, leaving 2" between each. Cut a shallow "X" into each cake, if desired.

Bake for about 15 minutes, or until lightly golden. Allow biscuits to cool on baking sheets for at least 5 minutes before moving, cool completely before serving.

If you want to get fancy with it, wrap them in leaves, and tie with twine. (I used collard greens).

* Choose your protein powder wisely! If it's something you don't like to drink, it'll make the bread taste weird.

Lembas

Raspberry Nectarine Muffins

When I first created this recipe, it was specifically to use up some of the raspberries we'd picked the day before. Our raspberry bushes had basically taken over the yard, and we had more berries than we knew what to do with.

I combined our fresh raspberries with my other favourite fruit, nectarines. They work so well together, especially with this less-sweet muffin. As they were baking, the whole kitchen smelled like I had raspberry jam cooking on the stove – amazing.

Makes 12 muffins

Light buckwheat flour	1 cup	250 ml
Sorghum flour	3/4 cup	175 ml
Potato flour	1/4 cup	50 ml
Coconut flour	1/4 cup	50 ml
Granulated sugar	3/4 cup	175 ml
Baking powder	2 tsp	10 ml
Salt	3/4 tsp	3 ml
Large eggs, lightly beaten	2	2
Milk	1 cup	250 ml
Honey	1/4 cup	50 ml
Butter, melted	½ cup	125 ml
Vanilla extract	1 tsp	5 ml
Nectarine, chopped	1	1
Fresh raspberries	3/4 cup	175 ml

Preheat oven to 375 F (190 C). Line 12 muffin cups with liners, or spray with baking spray.

In a large bowl, combine flours, sugar, baking powder and salt. Make a well in center of flour mixture; set aside.

In another bowl, combine eggs, milk, honey, melted butter, and vanilla extract, whisking until honey is well incorporated. Add egg mixture all at once to the flour mixture. Stir just until moistened (batter should be lumpy.) Gently fold in the nectarine and raspberries.

Divide batter between 12 prepared muffin cups, filling each to almost full.

Bake for 20 to 22 minutes or until golden and a wooden toothpick inserted in centers comes out clean. Cool in muffin cups on a wire rack for 5 minutes. Remove from muffin cups; serve warm.

Raspberry Nectarine Muffins

Breakfast Corn Muffins

These are less a "cupcake without icing" muffin, and more of a "entire breakfast in the palm of your hand" kind of muffin. Not only are these great fresh out of the oven, they make a great make-ahead breakfast for eating on the go the rest of the week.

Because corn meal is such a versatile base, the possibilities for these muffins are endless. (See below for a few suggestions to get you started!)

Makes 12 muffins

Cornmeal	3/4 cup	175 ml
Light Buckwheat flour	½ cup	125 ml
Sorghum flour	1/4 cup	50 ml
Tapioca starch	1/4 cup	50 ml
Masa Flour	1/4 cup	50 ml
Baking powder	1 tsp	5 ml
Salt	½ tsp	2 ml
Butter, softened	½ cup	125 ml
Granulated sugar	1/4 cup	50 ml
Honey	2 Tbsp	30 ml
Large eggs	2	2
Milk	2/3 cup	150 ml
Breakfast sausage, cooked	1 lb	500 g
Shredded cheddar cheese	1 cup	250 ml
Chopped green onions	1/4 cup	50 ml

Preheat oven to 400 F (200 C). Prepare muffin pan with cupcake liners or grease well.

Combine cornmeal, flours, starch, baking powder, and salt, stirring until well combined. Set aside.

In a large bowl, beat together butter, sugar, and honey until light and fluffy. Add eggs and milk, stirring carefully until well incorporated. Mix in the dry ingredients, stirring just until combined.

Spoon batter into prepared muffin pan. Bake for 22 to 25 minutes, until a knife or toothpick inserted into the center of a muffin comes out clean.

Variations:

• Jalapeño and Bacon: Swap out the sausage for 6 crumbled slices crispy bacon, add 1 finely chopped jalapeño.

• Sour Cream and Onion: Decrease milk to ¼ cup. Add ½ cup sour cream with the milk and eggs. You can take the sausage out, leave it in, or swap it for bacon!

Breakfast Corn Muffins

Breakfast Pizza

Growing up, this was my absolute favorite breakfast. It was a bastardized version of my grandma's baking powder biscuits recipe, and was definitely a treat. Much like the original, this is best served fresh out of the oven, hot!

Serves 4-6

Light buckwheat flour	1 cup	250 ml
Millet flour	½ cup	125 ml
Potato starch	1/4 cup	50 ml
Sweet rice flour	1/4 cup	50 ml
Baking Powder	3 tsp	15 ml
Salt	1 tsp	5 ml
Oregano	½ tsp	2 ml
Xanthan gum	½ tsp	2 ml
Shortening	½ cup	125 ml
Milk or buttermilk	1 cup	250 ml
Shredded sharp cheddar cheese	2 cups	500 ml
Cooked bacon, crumbled	12 strips	12 strips
Garlic salt	1/4 tsp	1 ml
Tomato, thinly sliced	1	1
Oregano, or to taste	3/4 tsp	3 ml

Preheat oven to 450 F (230 C)

In a medium sized bowl, mix together flours, potato starch, baking powder, salt, oregano, and xanthan gum.

Measure shortening into the same bowl, and cut into the dry ingredients using a pastry cutter or fork(s). The idea is to work it in until it's evenly distributed throughout, in very small pieces.

Add milk, stir just until dough comes together - you don't want to over handle it. Add ½ cup of the cheese, and about half of the bacon. Stir until incorporated.

On a greased baking sheet or pie plate, spread dough out, forming a crust that is of even thickness – between ½" – 3/4" thick. Sprinkle with garlic salt

Arrange tomato slices and crumbled bacon on the crust. Scatter remaining cheese over the entire pizza, then sprinkle remaining oregano on top.

Bake for 12-15 minutes, or until cooked through.

Breakfast Pizza

23

Broccoli Pancakes

If you're someone who doesn't like sweets in the morning, this will be right up your alley. It's not the kind of "blank slate" pancake you'd want to drown in syrup, it has a lot going on, on its own: a lot of flavour, texture, and colour. We like a little sour cream for balance and a little fat, but that's about it. The slight, softened crunch to the broccoli gives these a really satisfying texture.

Cooking the broccoli and onions can be done the night before, just leave them in the fridge until you're ready to make pancakes.

Note: If you want to elevate this dish a bit... cook them in bacon fat. Seriously.

Makes 7-8 pancakes

Finely chopped Broccoli Florets	2 cups	500 ml
Small onion, chopped	1	1
Olive oil	1 Tbsp	15 ml
Garlic cloves, pressed or minced	2	2
Light buckwheat flour	2/3 cup	150 ml
Sorghum flour	1/3 cup	75 ml
Baking powder	1 ½ tsp	7 ml
Salt	1/4 tsp	1 ml
Pepper	½ tsp	2 ml
Shredded Parmesan cheese	2/3 cup	150 ml
Large eggs, beaten	2	2
Buttermilk*	3/4 cup	175 ml
Vegetable oil or spray		
Sour cream		
Green onions		

Combine Broccoli, onion, and olive oil in a small fry pan. Sauté just until veggies start to soften. Add garlic, continue to cook for one more minute. Remove from heat, allow to cool to room temperature. You can leave them kind of chunky, or you can run them through a food processor to make them smaller and more uniform - we did.

In a medium sized bowl, combine flours, baking powder, salt, and pepper. Mix in Parmesan cheese and eggs until well distributed. Whisk in buttermilk until everything is more or less uniform, without over handling it. Stir in vegetable mix until well distributed.

Lightly oil your griddle or frying pan, preheat over medium heat. Scoop 1/4 cup amounts of batter onto the griddle. Gently spread batter out into a larger circle, about 4 – 4.5" in diameter. Cook until bubbles start popping through top surface. Flip, cook until done.

Serve with sour cream and sliced green onions

*If not buttermilk, use 3/4 cup milk, with 2 tsp lemon juice mixed in. Allow to sit for 5 minutes before using.

Broccoli Pancakes

Zucchini Loaf

This breakfast loaf has a great, soft texture, and a really nice taste. We love zucchini bread as something different - you don't really see it in stores, so it feels like a treat. Zucchini bread has a nice, mild, balanced flavour, vaguely reminiscent of pumpkin bread - not entirely surprising, as they're both squash!

Makes 1 loaf

Light buckwheat flour	3/4 cup	175 ml
Granulated sugar	3/4 cup	175 ml
Sorghum flour	½ cup	125 ml
Coconut flour	1/4 cup	50 ml
Baking soda	1 tsp	5 ml
Xanthan gum	1 tsp	5 ml
Baking powder	½ tsp	2 ml
Salt	3/4 tsp	3 ml
Ground cinnamon	½ tsp	2 ml
Ground cloves	pinch	pinch
Nutmeg	pinch	pinch
Butter, melted	½ cup	125 ml
Water	1/4 cup	50 ml
Large eggs	2	2 ml
Vanilla extract	1 tsp	5 ml
Grated fresh zucchini	1 ½ cups	375 ml
Walnuts or pecans	½ cup	125 ml

Preheat oven to 350 F (180 C). Grease 1 large loaf pan.

In a large bowl, whisk together flours, sugar, baking soda, xanthan gum, baking powder, salt, and spices.

Add butter, water, eggs and vanilla, mix until smooth. Add zucchini and nuts; Mix just until everything is well combined.

Pour batter into prepared loaf pan. Bake for about 1 hour, or until crust is a rich golden brown, and knife inserted into middle of loaf comes out clean.

Serve warm or cooled. Best served within 2-3 days.

Zucchini Loaf

Spiced Pumpkin Loaf

This breakfast loaf is fun, and is almost a dessert - it tastes like pumpkin pie! It's not overbearingly sweet, however.

If you have the patience, let a few slices dry out a bit and use it for a spiced French toast!

Makes 1 loaf

Light buckwheat flour	1 cup	250 ml
Light brown sugar, packed	1 cup	250 ml
Sorghum flour	½ cup	125 ml
Coconut flour	1/4 cup	50 ml
Baking powder	2 tsp	10 ml
Xanthan gum	1 tsp	5 ml
Baking soda	½ tsp	2 ml
Salt	3/4 tsp	3 ml
Cinnamon	1 tsp	5 ml
Ground ginger	½ tsp	2 ml
Nutmeg	½ tsp	2 ml
Ground cloves	1/4 tsp	1 ml
Butter, melted	1/4 cup	50 ml
Large eggs	2	2
Vanilla extract	1 tsp	5 ml
Canned pumpkin puree	1 cup	250 ml
Walnuts or pecans	½ cup	125 ml

Preheat oven to 350 F (180 C). Grease 1 large loaf pan.

In a large bowl, whisk together flours, brown sugar, baking powder, xanthan gum, baking soda, salt, and spices.

Add butter, eggs and vanilla, continue mixing until smooth. Add pumpkin puree and nuts, continue mixing just until everything is well combined.

Pour batter into prepared loaf pan. Bake for about 1 hour, or until crust is a rich golden brown, and knife inserted into middle of loaf comes out clean.

Serve warm, or cooled. Best served within 2-3 days.

Spiced Pumpkin Loaf

Pineapple Macadamia Loaf

The crunch of the macadamia nuts compliments the soft texture of this loaf so well. It has a subtle, tropical taste. Really nice - it tastes like summer!

Or, as my husband says... "It feels like eating a super soft cookie and not feeling guilty about it"

Makes 1 loaf

Light buckwheat flour	1 cup	250 ml
Granulated sugar	3/4 cup	175 ml
Sorghum flour	2/3 cup	150 ml
Coconut flour	1/4 cup	50 ml
Baking powder	2 tsp	10 ml
Xanthan gum	1 tsp	5 ml
Baking soda	½ tsp	2 ml
Salt	3/4 tsp	3 ml
Butter, melted	1/4 cup	50 ml
Large eggs	3	3
Vanilla extract	1 tsp	5 ml
Crushed pineapple	1 1/4 cup	300 ml
Chopped macadamia nuts	3/4 cup	175 ml

Preheat oven to 350 F (180 C). Grease 1 large loaf pan.

In a large bowl, whisk together flours, sugar, baking powder, xanthan gum, baking soda, and salt.

Add butter, eggs and vanilla, continue mixing until smooth. Add crushed pineapple, continue beating until well combined. Add macadamia nuts; mix just until everything is well combined.

Pour batter into prepared loaf pan. Bake for 50-60 minutes, or until crust is a rich golden brown, and knife inserted into middle of loaf comes out clean.

Serve warm, or cooled. Best served within 2-3 days.

Pineapple Macadamia Loaf

Spiced Carrot Loaf

This is great for when you're in the mood for dessert for breakfast- it tastes just like carrot cake! This loaf picks up some sweetness from the sorghum and coconut flours used, but isn't crazy sweet... so you can convince yourself it's a healthy breakfast food.

Makes 1 loaf

Light buckwheat flour	3/4 cup	175 ml
Brown sugar, packed	½ cup	125 ml
Granulated sugar	½ cup	125 ml
Sorghum flour	½ cup	125 ml
Coconut flour	1/4 cup	50 ml
Baking soda	1 tsp	5 ml
Baking powder	1 tsp	5 ml
Xanthan gum	1 tsp	5 ml
Ground cinnamon	1 tsp	5 ml
Nutmeg	½ tsp	2 ml
Salt	½ tsp	2 ml
Ground cloves	pinch	pinch
Butter, melted	½ cup	125 ml
Large eggs	3	3 ml
Vanilla extract	1 tsp	5 ml
Shredded carrots	1 cup	250 ml
Crushed pineapple	2/3 cup	150 ml
Walnuts	½ cup	125 ml
Raisins	3/4 cup	175 ml

Preheat oven to 350 F (180 C). Grease 1 large loaf pan.

In a large bowl, whisk together flours, sugars, baking soda, baking powder, xanthan gum, spices, and salt.

Add butter, eggs and vanilla, continue beating until smooth. Add carrots and pineapple, continue beating until well combined. Add walnuts and raisins; Mix just until everything is well combined.

Pour batter into prepared loaf pan. Bake for about 1 hour, or until crust is a rich golden brown, and knife inserted into middle of loaf comes out clean.

Serve warm, or cooled. Best served within 2-3 days.

Spiced Carrot Loaf

33

Cranberry Orange Loaf

This is a very festive and pretty loaf! I love the combo of the orange, cranberry, and pistachios. The warm gooey bits of cranberry in the slices remind us of muffins - and the batter for this could very easily be used to make muffins.

For muffins, scoop batter into greased muffin tins and bake for 20-22 minutes at 375 F (190 C)

Makes 1 loaf

Sorghum flour	1 cup	250 ml
Granulated sugar	1 cup	250 ml
Light buckwheat flour	½ cup	125 ml
Coconut flour	1/4 cup	50 ml
Baking powder	2 tsp	10 ml
Xanthan gum	1 tsp	5 ml
Salt	3/4 tsp	3 ml
Baking soda	½ tsp	2 ml
Butter, melted	1/4 cup	50 ml
Large eggs	2	2 ml
Vanilla extract	1 tsp	5 ml
Orange juice	1 cup	250 ml
Orange, zest of	1	1
Chopped fresh cranberries	1 ½ cups	375 ml
Walnuts, pecans, or pistachios	2/3 cups	150 ml

Preheat oven to 350 F (180 C). Grease 1 large loaf pan.

In a large bowl, whisk together flours, sugar, baking powder, xanthan gum, salt, and baking soda. Add butter, eggs and vanilla, continue mixing until smooth.

Add orange juice and zest, continue beating until well combined. Add cranberries and nuts; Mix just until everything is well combined.

Pour batter into prepared loaf pan. Bake for about 1 hour, or until crust is a rich golden brown, and knife inserted into middle of loaf comes out clean.

Serve warm, or cooled. Best served within 2-3 days.

Cranberry Orange Loaf

Cream of ... Not Wheat

Cream of ... Not Wheat

While oatmeal can still be an option for some people who have to stick to a gluten-free diet, certain other porridge-like breakfasts are now off the table.

This recipe - two ways! - was developed out of a yearning for a childhood favouite: A cereal named after the Red River, near where I grew up. As it was made from wheat and rye - along with flax - it was no longer an option for me. Still, I missed the toasty, nutty flavours of it!

This recipe can be made two ways: ground, or whole grain. Both are hearty, high fibre, flavourful ways to start the morning. They're especially great to start off a day spent outside in cold weather - they're filling, and really warm you up from the inside out.

Ground: Quick to cook up, with a porridge texture.

Whole Grain: Having the different sizes and textures of the different grains, is a lot of fun - they all have different sizes, shapes, and firmness. It gives the bowl an interesting character.

I like to mix up a batch of the grains and store them in an airtight container. This mixture is enough for 10-16 servings.

Whole buckwheat	1 cup	250 ml
Whole millet	1 cup	250 ml
Whole sorghum	1 cup	250 ml
Flax seeds	1 cup	250 ml
Teff grain	½ cup	125 ml
Amaranth	1/4 cup	50 ml

In batches, place grains in a large, dry nonstick pan. Cook over medium heat until fragrant. Remove from heat, mix all toasted grains together, allow to cool.

Ground Cereal: Process grains in a coffee grinder in small batches, until grains are slightly bigger than grains of sand.

To serve, measure 1/3 cup grain mixture per serving into a pot, top with 1 cup of water per serving. Bring to a boil, turn heat down and simmer until water is absorbed into the grains - about 10 minutes.

Whole Grain Cereal: Place half of the toasted, unprocessed grain mixture into a slow cooker. Add 8 cups of water, stir well, and cook on low overnight. (A crust of flax seeds may form, it's all good!). Serves 5-8.

To serve either way:

Season with salt, to taste. Spoon into bowls, and customize to taste: add milk, sugar, brown sugar, maple syrup, raisins, and or chopped nuts.

Bagels

Bagels

I'm not going to lie - these are really fussy to make. The dough behaves nothing at all like normal bagel dough does, and you will probably swear a lot while making a giant mess.

HOWEVER, they produce a bagel that is properly dense, chewy on the outside, and soft on the inside. You can eat them straight out of the oven with NO gumminess, or you can toast them after they've cooled off. While the dough is fragile and fussy to work with, the finished product is not - you can slather cream cheese on these babies without destroying them! Ugly bagels, sure... but tasty, tasty bagel goodness.

Makes 6 bagels

Warm water	1 1/4 cup	300 ml
Granulated sugar	2 Tbsp	30 ml
Active dry yeast	2 ½ tsp	22 ml
Light buckwheat flour	3/4 cup	175 ml
White rice flour	½ cup	125 ml
Unflavoured whey protein powder	½ cup	125 ml
Potato starch	½ cup	125 ml
Sweet rice flour	1/4 cup	50 ml
Tapioca starch	1/4 cup	50 ml
Xanthan gum	2 tsp	10 ml
Salt	1 tsp	5 ml
Baking powder	½ tsp	2 ml
Vegetable oil	1/4 cup	50 ml
Large egg	1	1
Nonstick pan spray		
Potato starch	1/3 cup	75 ml
Water	3 quarts	3 L
Baking soda	1 Tbsp	15 ml
Large egg	1	1
Cold water	1 Tbsp	15 ml

Optional toppings: Sesame seeds, poppy seeds, dried onion flakes, etc.

Combine warm water with sugar, stir until sugar is almost dissolved. Add yeast, stirring until incorporated. Set aside in a warm place for 10 minutes, or until foamy.

In a large bowl, combine flours, protein powder, starches, xanthan gum, salt, and baking powder. Add oil and egg, stirring until well distributed. Pour in yeast mixture, stirring until well combined - it will be VERY wet.

Use pan spray to generously grease a large, clean metal or glass bowl. Add dough to the bowl, loosely cover with plastic wrap, set aside in a warm spot to rise for an hour or so, until doubled in size.

Once the dough has doubled in size:

Line baking sheet with parchment paper, spray generously with pan spray, set aside.

Stir remaining potato starch into the dough. Stir until no longer *super* sticky - it'll still be a little sticky. Use a little more potato starch if needed. Spray hands with pan spray, divide the mixture into 6 equal sized balls.

Roll one section of dough into a ball. Flatten it out slightly, before poking a finger though the middle. Place on prepared baking sheet. Repeat with remaining sections of dough. With wet hands, smooth the outside of each bagel, and stretch the inner hole a bit. Cover loosely with plastic wrap, allow to rise in a warm place for another hour.

Preheat oven to 350 F (180 C), Line a separate baking sheet with parchment paper, spray generously with pan spray. Bring a large pot of water to a gentle simmer, stir in baking soda.

Carefully cut the parchment paper between the bagels, to separate them - you don't want to jostle them too much, or even really touch them.

One at a time, carefully transfer the bagels to the pot of water. Lift one by the parchment paper, and gently turn it over into the water, removing the parchment paper as you go. (It should easily release). Depending on the size of your pot, you can boil 2-3 bagels at a time.

Boil bagels for 1-2 minutes on each side - a longer boil will result in a chewier bagel. Gently stir as they boil, to ensure that the entire surface of each is in contact with the water at some point.

Use a slotted spoon to carefully transfer each bagel to prepared baking sheet.

Whisk egg together with 1 Tbsp of water, brush over the tops and sides of each bagel. Sprinkle bagels with any toppings you would like to use (optional).

Bake for 35-40 minutes, until golden brown.

Serve hot, or allow to fully cool before transferring to an airtight container or baggies. Use within 2-3 days for best results.

Cheese Crackers

Appetizers & Sides

Cheese Crackers

If you like Cheese, It's clear you'll want to make these... if you know what I'm saying.

The use of good cheese in these really elevates them over the source material, with a cleaner, clearer cheese taste. These puff up significantly in the oven, yielding very flaky, buttery crackers. You may want to double the batch, as they go fast!

Makes about 175 Cheese Crackers

Corn starch	½ cup	125 ml
Millet flour	½ cup	125 ml
Sorghum flour	1/4 cup	50 ml
Light buckwheat flour	1/4 cup	50 ml
Salt	½ tsp	2 ml
Xanthan gum	½ tsp	2 ml
Shredded sharp cheddar cheese	8 oz	250 g
Shredded Parmesan cheese	½ cup	125 ml
Cold butter, chopped	½ cup	125 ml
Cold water	1/3 cup	75 ml
Additional corn starch for rolling		

Measure corn starch, flours, salt, and xanthan gum into the bowl of your food processor, blitz to combine.

Add cheeses and butter, blitz a few times until mixture resembles gravel. Stream in cold water as you run the food processor, just long enough to start to bring it together as a dough – you may need to use a little more or less water. Do NOT over-process it!

Remove dough from processor, knead lightly to bring it together as a ball. Wrap in plastic film, chill for 1 hour.

Preheat oven to 375 F (190 C) . Line 2 baking sheets with parchment paper.

Scatter some corn starch over your - clean! - work surface. Roll dough out 1/4" thick, cut into 1" square pieces.   Use a chopstick or small straw to poke a hole in the center of each piece, carefully transfer to lined baking sheets.

Bake for 11-12 minutes, or until golden and puffy. Allow to cool to room temperature before storing in an airtight container.

Butter Crackers

Can we talk about how terrible store bought gluten free crackers are ... And at what a cost! Flavourless, terrible texture, and just not anything that really adds anything to the cheese you want to serve on them, you know? Also, you definitely need to serve cheese on them, because they're not the kind of thing you'd want to just snack on a handful of, bare.

These are my answer to those abominations. These are really flaky and buttery, will hold up to whatever you serve on them, and not turn to dust as you bite in. The flavour is amazing, and they come together really quickly and easily.

I like to use Wilton's 6 piece "Double Cut-Outs Set" of fondant/cookie cutters. Each cutter has a straight edge side, and a fluted side - and one of them is the perfect size for butter crackers.

Makes 90-100 crackers

Sorghum flour	½ cup	125 ml
Light buckwheat flour	½ cup	125 ml
Millet flour	½ cup	125 ml
Corn starch	½ cup	125 ml
Baking powder	1 Tbsp	15 ml
Granulated sugar	2 tsp	10 ml
Xanthan gum	1 tsp	5 ml
Salt, plus additional	3/4 tsp	3 ml
Baking soda	1/4 tsp	1 ml
Cold butter, divided	3/4 cup	175 ml
Cold water	½ cup	125 ml

Measure flours, corn starch, baking powder, sugar, xanthan gum, salt, and baking soda into the bowl of your food processor, blitz to combine.

Add ½ cup of the butter, blitz a few times until mixture resembles gravel. Stream in cold water as you run the food processor, just long enough to start to bring it together as a dough – you may need to use a little more or less water. Do NOT over-process it!

Remove dough from processor, knead lightly to bring it together as a ball. Wrap in plastic film, chill for 1 hour.

Preheat oven to 375 F (190 C) . Line 2 baking sheets with parchment paper.

Scatter some corn starch over your - clean! - work surface. Roll dough out 1/4" thick, cut into rounds. Prick each cracker with a fork, carefully transfer to prepared baking sheets. Bake for about 15 minutes, or until golden and puffy.

Melt remaining butter. Brush over hot crackers, sprinkle with salt. Allow to cool completely, before storing in an airtight container.

Butter Crackers

Grainy Crackers

I modelled these crackers after my favourite glutteny ones, which I've missed terribly. Full of flavour - all kinds of seeds, different grains, etc. While I can't use some of the ingredients in the original that contribute to the complex flavour - like rye and barley - many of the source material ingredients ARE gluten free. I've added flax meal to take the place of some of the gluten-based flavour, and a little amaranth for a savoury kick. Toasting the initial batch of ingredients not only improves the flavour and complexity of the overall recipe, it also serves to take the place of the malting of certain ingredients in the source material.

Oat bran	1/4 cup	50 ml
Sunflower seeds	1/4 cup	50 ml
Whole millet	4 tsp	20 ml
Flax meal	1 Tbsp	15 ml
Sesame seeds	2 tsp	10 ml
Mustard seeds	1 tsp	5 ml
Poppy seeds	1 tsp	5 ml
Millet flour	½ cup	125 ml
Light buckwheat flour	½ cup	125 ml
Corn starch	½ cup	125 ml
Amaranth flour	1/4 cup	50 ml
Baking powder	1 Tbsp	15 ml
Granulated sugar	2 tsp	10 ml
Xanthan gum	1 tsp	5 ml
Salt, plus additional	3/4 tsp	3 ml
Pepper	1/4 tsp	1 ml
Baking soda	1/4 tsp	1 ml
Cold butter, divided	3/4 cup	175 ml
Cold water	2/3 cup	150 ml

Combine oat bran, seeds, millet and flax meal in a large nonstick pan. Toast over medium heat until fragrant. Add to a food processor, along with flours, corn starch, baking powder, sugar, xanthan gum, salt, pepper, and baking soda, blitz to combine.

Add ½ cup of the butter, blitz a few times until mixture resembles gravel. Stream in cold water as you run the food processor, just long enough to start to bring it together as a dough – you may need to use a little more or less water. Do NOT over-process it! Remove dough from processor, knead lightly to bring it together as a ball. Wrap in plastic film, chill for 1 hour.

Preheat oven to 375 F (190 C) . Line 2 baking sheets with parchment paper. Scatter some corn starch over your - clean! - work surface. Roll dough out 1/4" thick, cut into rounds. Prick each cracker with a fork, carefully transfer to prepared baking sheets.

Bake for about 15 minutes, or until golden and puffy. Melt remaining butter, brush over hot crackers, sprinkle with salt. Allow to cool completely, before storing in an airtight container.

Grainy Crackers

Spaetzle

The texture on these little German dumplings is really fun - it's like pasta, but not really. As my husband likes to say, it's like the difference between ice cream, and Dippin' Dots (TM) - just fun to eat. These work up incredibly quickly and easily - you can be eating less than 20 minutes after deciding that you would like to make a batch!   Dressing it with something simple like dill and butter works really well. While many people think of pastas as being a blank canvas for sauces, this really diverges from that in that it stands on its own really well as a dumpling - it has good flavour. For even more flavour, feel free to cook these in chicken stock, rather than water.

White rice flour	½ cup	125 ml
Millet flour	1/4 cup	50 ml
Sweet rice flour	1/4 cup	50 ml
Tapioca starch	2 Tbsp	30 ml
Xanthan gum	½ tsp	2 ml
Salt, plus additional	½ tsp	2 ml
Pepper	1/4 tsp	1 ml
Ground nutmeg	pinch	pinch
Milk	½ cup	125 ml
Large eggs, beaten	3	3
Nonstick spray		
Butter, melted	2 Tbsp	30 ml

In a large mixing bowl, whisk together flours, starch, xanthan gum, salt, pepper, and nutmeg. Add eggs and milk, a little at a time, whisking until very smooth. Cover with plastic wrap, set aside for 15 minutes.

In a large pot, combine about a gallon of water with a Tbsp or so of salt. Bring to a gentle boil.

Remove the hopper from your spaetzle maker, if applicable, and spray both pieces well with pan spray. Reassemble, and place over pot of water. Carefully fill the hopper of your spaetzle maker with dough, and move the hopper slowly back and forth. As the hopper empties, add more dough. Once all of the dough is used, give the pot a gentle stir.

As dumplings start to float, start timing - you'll want them to cook for 2 minutes after floating. Once the time is up, use a slotted spoon or wire basket to skim the floating ones from the pot, rinse with hot water, and transfer to a clean bowl. Toss with butter to prevent sticking.

Once all dumplings are cooked and coated with butter, you can serve them as-is, or finish them off in one of the following ways:

Sautéed with herbs: Transfer cooked spaetzle to a large nonstick pan, sauté with additional butter. Sprinkle finely chopped fresh parsley or dill over it, and serve.

Bacon: In a large nonstick pan, cook chopped bacon and sliced onions together until bacon is cooked and onions are starting to caramelize. Add spaetzle to the pan, sauté until heated through. Serve hot.

Spaetzle

Tabbouleh

I love quinoa. The taste is decent, and it's a fun texture to eat. When I first started eating it about a decade ago, it was mostly in soups, as a healthier (and more fun!) alternative to noodles or rice. Sometimes I'd serve it on its own, almost like a rice... but it was only a few years ago that I started using it in what's now my favourite application for quinoa: tabbouleh!

Even before discovering that I need to be gluten-free, I found that I actually preferred the taste and texture of quinoa to the traditional bulghur wheat used in tabbouleh.

Beyond being inherently gluten-free, this recipe was created with another need in mind – my husband's utter hatred of tomatoes. I wanted a tabbouleh I could share with him, rather than hoard for myself. So: red peppers. They work really well with the other flavours and textures.

Makes about 6-8 servings

Uncooked quinoa	1 cup	250 ml
Red bell peppers, seeded and chopped	2	2
Cucumbers, seeded, and chopped	2	2
Green onions, thinly sliced	4	4
Parsley, chopped	1 bunch	1 bunch
Fresh mint, chopped	1 bunch	1 bunch
Lemons, zest and juice of	1-2	1-2
Olive oil	1/3 cup	75 ml
Garlic cloves , pressed or minced	3-4	3-4
Salt	2 tsp	10 ml
Pepper	1 tsp	5 ml

In a pot, bring quinoa and 2 cups hot water to a boil. Cover, reduce heat to low, and simmer for 10-15 minutes or until all the water is absorbed. Stir well, remove from heat, and transfer to a mixing bowl to cool a bit.

After 10-15 minutes, toss to fluff, then allow to cool to room temperature.

Once cooled, add peppers, cucumbers, green onions, parsley, mint, and lemon zest. Stir to combine.

In a separate bowl, combine lemon juice with remaining ingredients, whisking to combine well. Pour over salad, toss to combine. Cover and chill for at least 3 hours before serving.

Tabbouleh

Scalloped Potatoes

One day, while shopping for the cheapest, stinkiest tuna we could find (cats LOVE it), I noticed something from the corner of my eye: Jalapeno cheddar instant scalloped potatoes. It stopped me dead in my tracks- why hadn't I ever thought to put jalapeno in scalloped potatoes? It was an epiphany!

With heavy cream leftover from other projects waiting for us at home, I decided to develop my own version… it was amazing. The sauce almost didn't make it to the potatoes, from uh.. "quality control". Also, the smell coming out of the oven was maddening. Why is it that the recipes that put out the most tantalizing smells seem to start doing so the earliest in their cook times, and have the LONGEST cook times?

Makes ~ 8 servings

Large jalapenos, seeded and finely chopped	2-3	2-3
Small onion, finely chopped	1	1
Garlic cloves, pressed or minced	2	2
Butter	1 Tbsp	15 ml
White rice flour	1/4 cup	50 ml
Gluten-free beer (Or chicken broth)	1 cup	250 ml
Heavy cream (or Half and Half)	3 cups	750 ml
Shredded Monterey Jack cheese	1 cup	250 ml
Salt and pepper		
Red potatoes, washed	4 lbs	2 kg
Nonstick spray		
Shredded sharp cheddar cheese	1 cup	250 ml

Preheat oven to 400 F (200 C).

In a medium or large saucepan, combine jalapenos, onion, garlic, and butter. Sauté for a few minutes, until onion and peppers soften up a little. Add rice flour, whisk until well distributed and free of clumps.

Add beer, whisking well until smooth. Add heavy cream, continuing to whisk, until smooth. Bring to a boil. As mixture starts to boil, add shredded jack cheese, continue stirring until melted and smooth. Remove from heat, season with salt and pepper to taste.

Peel potatoes if you like – we don't bother, we like the skins! – and slice VERY thinly. Spray a 9 x 13 baking dish, and layer about a third of the potatoes in there. Pour a third of the sauce over it, tilting the pan to let it seep through the layers. Layer another third of the potatoes, pouring another third of the sauce over it. Repeat one more time, using up the remaining potatoes and sauce. Cover with foil.

Bake for 1 hour. Remove foil, return to oven for another 20 minutes. Remove from oven, scatter cheddar cheese evenly over the top, and return to the oven for another 10 minutes, or until nicely browned. Serve hot!

Scalloped Potatoes

Spicy Artichoke Cheese Dip

There's a local restaurant that makes a spicy artichoke cheese dip that I LOVED before my gluten problems. Aside from the fact that it's not gluten-free AND is served with bread, the restaurant is incredibly noisy - all good reasons to take some inspiration and make my own!

We decided to make our home version creamier and cheesier than the source material, and added white wine and provolone. The end result is nothing short of spectacular - definitely the best artichoke dip I've ever had!

This makes a fair amount of dip, so it's great for parties. If you – like us – only have a couple of people to feed, never fear – it reheats well, and it's just way too addictive to go to waste. You will plow through a batch in no time!

Serves about 6 as an appetizer

14 oz cans artichoke hearts	2	2
Red bell pepper, seeded and chopped	1	1
Jalapeno peppers, finely chopped*	3	3
Olive oil	1 Tbsp	15 ml
Garlic cloves, pressed or minced	3	3
Dry white wine	½ cup	125 ml
Cream cheese, softened	12 oz	375 g
Grated Parmesan cheese, divided	1 1/4 cup	300 ml
Provolone cheese, shredded	8 oz	250 g
Fresh lemon zest	1 tsp	5 ml
Pepper	½ tsp	2 ml
Salt		

Heat broiler to high. Drain and chop artichoke hearts.

In a large saucepan over medium high heat, cook artichoke hearts, peppers, olive oil, and garlic together for a few minutes, until peppers soften a little. Add white wine, cook for another minute.

Carefully mix in softened cream cheese, stirring gently until smooth and well incorporated. Continue heating, stirring frequently, until cheese starts to bubble. Add in 1 cup of the Parmesan, all of the provolone, as well as the lemon zest and pepper. Stir constantly, until all cheese is melted and smooth. Season with salt, to taste.

Transfer mixture to an oven safe glass baking dish, such as Pyrex – we used a large Pyrex loaf pan. Sprinkle with remaining 1/4 cup of Parmesan cheese.

Broil for a few minutes, until the top of the dip is as browned as you'd like it. Serve hot, with gluten-free bagel chips, corn chips, and/or veggies.

*You can remove the seeds and ribs if you'd like a more mild dip – we left it all in.

Spicy Artichoke Cheese Dip

Samosas

Samosas

As someone who was introduced to samosas as a teen and has loved them ever since, losing them to my gluten allergy was painful! I had to fix that.

After some experimentation, I came up with a great samosa dough recipe - it had a great texture, and the taste really worked well with the ingredients. Though Garbanzo flour can be too aggressive for a lot of uses, it works really well with Indian food.

Visually, these end up looking a little different because of the way the starch fries up - staying white, while the rest of the dough browns well - but the taste was perfect. The cilantro mint chutney is quick and easy to make, and works really well with the flavours in the samosa..

Being able to have to freshly made samosas at home, not even having to go to a restaurant, was amazing! They reheated well, too.

There are many different ways to assemble samosas - Many people do flat triangle pockets, many do it more like a pyramid. I first had it as a pyramid, so that's how I do it.

Makes 16 large samosas

Russet potatoes, washed	3	3
Onion, finely chopped	1	1
Large carrot, peeled and grated	1	1
Olive oil	1 Tbsp	15 ml
Garlic cloves, minced or pressed	2	2
Ginger paste	1 tsp	5 ml
Curry powder	1 Tbsp	15 ml
Garam masala	1 tsp	5 ml
Ground coriander	½ tsp	2 ml
Cayenne	½ tsp	2 ml
Cumin	1/4 tsp	1 ml
Lemon juice	2 Tbsp	30 ml
Water	2 Tbsp	30 ml
Frozen peas, thawed	1 cup	250 ml
Chopped cilantro	2 Tbsp	30 ml
Salt and pepper		

White rice flour	3/4 cup	175 ml
Light buckwheat flour	3/4 cup	175 ml
Garbanzo flour	½ cup	125 ml
Sweet rice flour	1/4 cup	50 ml
Potato starch	1/4 cup	50 ml
Xanthan gum	2 tsp	10 ml
Salt	½ tsp	2 ml
Cream cheese, softened	8 oz	250 g
Cold butter	½ cup	125 ml
Large egg	1	1
Cold water	½ cup	125 ml

Peel potatoes, cut into large chunks. Boil until just tender, about 15 minutes.

Sauté onion and carrot in olive oil until tender. Add garlic and ginger, cook for another minute. Add potatoes, spices, lemon juice, and water; mash lightly, stir to combine everything. Add peas and cilantro, season with salt and pepper to taste. Set aside.

Measure flours, potato starch, xanthan gum, and salt into the bowl of your food processor, blitz to combine. Add cream cheese, butter, and egg, blitz a few times until mixture resembles gravel. Stream in cold water as you run the food processor, just long enough to start to bring it together as a dough – you may need to use a little more or less water. Do NOT over-process it!

Remove dough from processor, knead lightly to bring it together as a ball. Wrap in plastic film, rest on counter for 1 hour.

To assemble:

Start heating your oil to 350 F (180 C) – you'll want at least 2-3" of oil in your pot or deep fryer. Divide dough into 8 equal pieces.

Scatter some potato starch over your - clean! - work surface. Roll one piece of dough out to a 6-7" square-ish piece. Cut in half, diagonally.

Working with one of the two cut pieces, lightly wet the straight edge you just cut. Fold the dough in half along that straight edge, so the wet edge meets up with itself. Press and crimp to seal.

Pick up the piece of dough, gently separating formed "pocket" into a cone shape. Stuff with filling, then flip the uncut corner edge over to meet the cut edges. Pinch edges to seal. Repeat with the other cut piece, and remaining dough balls

Fry a few at a time - turning every few minutes - until crispy and golden, about 8-10 minutes. Use a slotted spoon to transfer fried samosas to platter lined with paper towels. Serve hot, with cilantro-mint chutney.

Cilantro-Mint Chutney

Fresh cilantro	2 bunches	2 bunches
Fresh mint leaves	2 bunches	2 bunches
Jalapeno, chopped	1	1
Juice of ½ large lime		
Salt	½ tsp	2 ml
Cumin	1 tsp	5 ml
Granulated sugar	1 tsp	5 ml

Measure everything but the cilantro into a food processor, pulse into finely chopped – almost a paste. Add a handful of cilantro, pulse til combined. Add the rest of the cilantro, pulse until well chopped and combined. Cover and refrigerate until use.

Brie Bites

Sometimes, inspiration comes from the weirdest places. During a chatroom discussion on poutine one night, I was asked if poutine used cheddar curds, or some other kind. My husband was feeling troll-y, so he replied "Brie curds", knowing full well that such a thing could never even exist, technically. Well, one thing led to another, and we decided engage in some sacrilege - battering and deep frying brie. Rather than a normal beer batter, I decided that this needed a white wine batter, with a little garlic.

Oh, they were *fantastic*. The first time we made this, we used the cheapest brie we could find - we were feeling a bit guilty about what we were about to do to it! It turned out so well, we tried it again with a name brand, mid grade brie. We definitely recommend going with a nicer brie, rather than the cheapest you can find. It really did make a difference, and the finished product is SO good, I don't think it ended up counting as sacrilege. Try to use a pretty fresh brie - you want it relatively firm. Once the center starts liquifying, it would be very difficult to work with.

Serves 4

Frying oil		
Garbanzo flour	½ cup	125 ml
White rice flour	½ cup	125 ml
Baking powder	1 tsp	5 ml
Salt	½ tsp	2 ml
Pepper	1/4 tsp	1 ml
Garlic powder	1/4 tsp	1 ml
Large egg, beaten	1	1
Dry white wine	3/4 cup	175 ml
Brie	1 lb	500 g
Corn starch, for dredging	½ cup	125 ml
Apricot preserves for serving		

Start heating your oil to 350 F (180 C) - you'll want at least 2-3" of oil in your pot or deep fryer.

In a large bowl, combine flours, baking powder, salt, pepper, and garlic powder. Add egg and wine, stir well to form a thick batter. All batter to sit for 15 minutes or so, to soften the flours.

Carefully cut the rind off the brie - freezing it for a few minutes can make this easier. Slice into small wedges. Gently dredge cheese wedges in corn starch, shaking excess back into the bowl. One piece at a time, dip into batter, allowing excess batter to drip back into bowl for a few seconds, before carefully transferring to heated oil.

Fry for a few minutes on each side, until golden brown and cooked through. Use a slotted metal spoon to transfer fried cheese to paper towels. Allow oil to come back up to temperature between batches. Serve hot, with apricot preserves.

Brie Bites

Pyrizhky

Pyrizhky

Growing up, I loved Sauerkraut buns… soft little bready balls of joy that would show up at family gatherings. Though we're not Ukrainian ourselves, growing up in Winnipeg meant that many of the traditional foods from other cultures – especially Ukrainian – were pretty ubiquitous. Bacon, onion, and sauerkraut is a pretty genius filling, so it's no wonder that these were super popular back home. I'm kind of surprised that it seems like none of my American friends have ever heard of them!

While preparing for Pi Day a few years ago, I decided that it was time to develop a recipe for a gluten-free version. These aren't QUITE as soft as the original – and the technique is different for putting them together… but they are full of flavour, inside and out. The bread has a great texture, and they're easy to make.

Makes about 25 buns

Warm water	½ cup	125 ml
Granulated sugar	1 tsp	5 ml
Active dry yeast	2 ½ tsp	12 ml
Light buckwheat flour	1 ½ cup+	375 ml+
Sorghum flour	3/4 cup	175 ml
Amaranth flour	½ cup	125 ml
Millet flour	½ cup	125 ml
Corn starch	1/4 cup	50 ml
Sweet rice flour	1/4 cup	50 ml
Tapioca starch	2 Tbsp	30 ml
Xanthan gum	3 tsp	15 ml
Salt	1 tsp	5 ml
Vegetable oil	½ cup	125 ml
Large eggs, beaten	3	3
Sour cream	1 cup	250 ml
Bacon, chopped	½ lb	250 g
Small onion, chopped	1	1
Saurkraut, well drained	1 cup	250 ml
Salt		
Pepper		
Melted butter	1/4 cup	50 ml

Gently mix together warm water, sugar, and yeast. Allow to sit for 10 minutes.

In a large bowl, mix together 1 cup of the buckwheat flour, remaining flours, starches, xanthan gum and salt. Form a well in the middle, and pour oil, eggs, and sour cream into it. Mix well, then add the yeasty water. Mix until everything is well incorporated - it will be a bit wet. Place dough in a large, greased bowl. Cover and allow to rise somewhere warm for 1 hour.

As you are waiting for the dough to rise, prepare the filling:

Cook bacon & onion until bacon is cooked, but not crispy. Add sauerkraut to the pan, cook and stir well until bacon fat is absorbed and everything is heated through. Season with salt and pepper to taste. Let cool.

One the hour rise is up, mix remaining ½ cup buckwheat flour into the dough. Pinch off a walnut sized piece of dough, and work into a circle as a test. If dough is too wet to work with, add a little more buckwheat flour. You want it more wet than normal dough, but still workable. Let stand for another 10 minutes.

Assemble the sauerkraut balls*:

Divide dough into a bunch of walnut sized pieces – about 25 of them.

One at a time, flatten a piece of dough into a circle approximately 3" across – I like to do this in the palm of one hand. Place a 1 Tbsp mound of filling in the center of the circle. Carefully pull up the edge of the circle up and around the filling, sealing the filling in (like a drawstring bag). Roll around between your hands a bit to get a uniform spherical shape, repeat with the rest of the dough/filling.

Get a large pot of water boiling, gently boil buns for 2 minutes each. Remove from water, arrange on parchment lined baking sheet, leaving at least 2" between dough balls.

Loosely cover baking sheets with plastic wrap, and allow to rise another hour.

Heat oven to 425 F (220 C). Remove plastic wrap from baking sheets, bake for 15 minutes, or until lightly golden. Remove from oven and brush liberally with melted butter, then broil for another 3 minutes or so, until nicely brown.

Best served hot - fresh out of the oven or reheated... IF they last that long.

* Note: I like to wear latex gloves for assembly. Spraying hands with pan spray is also a good idea.

Lefse

I'd honestly never even heard of lefse before moving to Minnesota, but it is a *thing* here. Even my not-Scandinavian-at-all husband has holiday memories of Lefse.

Lefse is a potato based flat bread - somewhere between a tortilla and a crepe - primarily served during two main seasons here: State Fair, and Christmas.

It's served warm or room temperature, in a variety of ways: Spread with butter, sprinkled with cinnamon sugar and rolled up, rolled up with cheeses and/or deli meats, or - my favourite - spread with a mixture of cream cheese and shredded vegetables and rolled up.

The "rolled up" seems to be a default or requirement, so we needed a dough that wouldn't crack when rolled, which we were able to do here!

Now, purists will tell you that you need a special lefse griddle, and a "lefse stick", but you really don't. You do, however, need some sort of large flat cooking surface - a normal griddle or large nonstick pan - that can get VERY hot - you want to aim for 400 F (200 C).

Makes 20 lefse, about 5" x 8" each

Russet potatoes	2 lbs	1 kg
Heavy whipping cream	½ cup	125 ml
Butter	1/4 cup	50 ml
Granulated sugar	2 tsp	10 ml
Salt	2 tsp	10 ml
Sorghum flour	½ cup	125 ml
Light buckwheat flour	1/3 cup	75 ml
White rice flour	1/4 cup	50 ml
Sweet rice flour	1/4 cup	50 ml
Tapioca starch	2 Tbsp	30 ml
Xanthan gum	1 tsp	5 ml
Large egg	1	1
Corn or potato starch for rolling		

Clean and peel potatoes, cut into chunks that are roughly equal in size - you want them to cook evenly. Boil until tender, about 20 minutes. Drain well - you do NOT want wet potatoes for this.

Use a potato ricer to rice potatoes while hot; measure out 4 cups of riced potatoes into a large bowl.

Mix whipping cream, butter, sugar, and salt into hot riced potatoes, stirring to melt the butter and combine ingredients well. Cool potato mixture to room temperature. Once potatoes are THOROUGHLY cool - I'm not kidding - you can proceed.

In a separate bowl, combine flours, starch, and xanthan gum. Add to bowl of cooled potatoes along with the egg, mix well to combine. Knead gently to bring a nice dough together. Cover with plastic wrap, allow to sit for 30 minutes. (If not using immediately, you can refrigerate overnight)

Pinch off golf ball sized pieces of dough, roll into balls. Cover with plastic wrap, chill for 10 minutes.

Scatter some corn or potato starch over your - clean! - work surface. Roll a ball out to an oblong shape, about 1/8" thick, (or slightly thinner, if you can). Use as little starch as you can to prevent sticking, you don't want a lot of excess starch on the rounds when you cook them.

Heat your pan or griddle to around 400 F (200 C). Cook your first lefse until bubbly and blistered. Flip, repeat on the other side.

Transfer cooked lefse to a plate, cover with a clean dish cloth, and repeat with remaining balls of lefse.

Serve warm, or cool completely before wrapping in plastic to refrigerate or freeze.

Lefse

Pizza Rolls

My husband loves those frozen pizza rolls you can get at any grocery store as a guilty pleasure, and - to be honest - once in a while I'd crave them too. Those chewy little pillows of pizza-like filling can be kind of nostalgic and fun!

Whether you're making these for a kid or an adult, they will satisfy cravings for that kind of thing. Use a nice cheese and good quality sauce to really elevate this - they can be better than the source material!

Makes 50-60 pizza rolls

Sour cream	½ cup	125 ml
Large eggs	2	2
Warm milk	1/4 cup	50 ml
Vegetable oil	1/4 cup	50 ml
Tapioca starch	2/3 cup	150 ml
Sorghum flour	½ cup	125 ml
Amaranth flour	½ cup	125 ml
Sweet rice flour	1/3 cup	75 ml
Corn starch	1/3 cup	75 ml
Potato starch	1/3 cup	75 ml
Xanthan gum	2 tsp	10 ml
Baking powder	1 tsp	5 ml
Salt	½ tsp	2 ml
Cold butter	½ cup	125 ml
Pepperoni	4 oz	125 g
Shredded cheese	8 oz	250 g
Pizza sauce of choice	~2/3 cup	~150 ml
Corn starch		
Large egg	1	1
Cold water	1 tsp	5 ml

In a mixing bowl, whisk together sour cream, eggs, milk and oil until well combined.

In a food processor, blitz together starches, flours, xanthan gum, baking powder, and salt until well combined. Add butter, blitz until mixture resembles gravel. Add wet mix, blitz just long enough to allow a sticky dough to come together. Wrap dough in plastic film, allow to rest on counter for 45 minutes. While waiting, work on the filling:

Finely chop pepperoni, place in a bowl with shredded cheese, stir to combine. Add just enough pizza sauce to barely bind the ingredients together. Wrap with plastic, chill until use.

Line a baking sheet with parchment paper, set aside. Dust work surface lightly with corn starch.

Roll dough out very thin - about 1/8 of an inch thick. Using a pizza wheel or sharp knife, cut dough into 1.5" wide strips. Cut those strips into 4" long pieces. Place about 1 tsp of filling in the middle of each piece.

Whisk together egg and water, use a pastry brush to paint a thin line of egg mixture along all 4 edges of each piece. Fold the two short ends in to the middle, overlapping slightly. Press down on all edges, taking care to push out any excess air.

Transfer all pizza rolls to baking sheet.

Get a large pot of water JUST to the point of gently bubbling - you don't want violent bubbles, or it'll rip apart your rolls. In small batches, poach the pizza rolls just until they float. Transfer cooked rolls back to the baking sheet to drain off.

Heat oil to 350 F (180 C). You can use a deep fryer, or a heavy pan. If not using a deep fryer, use a deep, heavy pot, filled to at least 2" deep. Line a clean baking sheet with 2 layers of paper towels.

Once oil reaches temperature, carefully fry pizza rolls in small batches until nicely browned and crispy. This should take about 1-2 minutes per side. Transfer fried pizza rolls to baking sheet to drain, serve hot.

Pizza Rolls

Mushroom Croquettes

These prompted the question "Is there a term for that... bar food satisfaction of anything deep fried?" from my husband. Not too sure on that, but these go way beyond bar food satisfaction. The creamy mushroom filling is packed with flavour, and it perfectly complemented by the crunch of the crust.

Be forewarned - like many fried items, these are definitely best when fresh. The coating is awesomely crisp fresh out of the fryer, but will go soggy if refrigerated.

Makes about 30 croquettes

Potato starch	½ cup	125 ml
Milk	2/3 cup	150 ml
Olive oil	2 Tbsp	30 ml
Mushrooms, finely chopped	1 lb	500 g
Small onion, finely chopped	½	½
Garlic cloves, pressed or minced	2	2
Dry white wine	1/4 cup	50 ml
Shredded Swiss cheese	½ cup	125 ml
Salt		
Pepper		
Cornstarch	½ cup	125 ml
Large eggs	3	3
Corn flake crumbs	2 cups	500 ml
Vegetable oil		

In a small bowl, whisk together potato starch and milk until smooth with no lumps, set aside

In a large pan, cook olive oil, mushrooms, and onion - stirring frequently - until vegetables are soft. Add garlic, stirring well to evenly distribute. Slowly add wine to the pot, whisking until smooth. Allow mixture to cook - stirring frequently - for 2 minutes.

Slowly add milk mixture to pan, continue whisking until everything is smooth and well incorporated. Add cheese, stir well, and continue to cook until cheese is completely melted throughout. Simmer until mixture thickens - it should be VERY thick. Season with salt and pepper, to taste. Remove from heat, cool to room temperature, and then chill until cold and firm - at least 2 hours.

Roll mushroom mixture into walnut sized balls, return to the fridge to chill for another 20 minutes or so.

Line one baking sheet with 2-3 layers of paper towels, and another with a layer of parchment paper, set aside.

Arrange 3 bowls on your work surface. Put the cornstarch in the first, the eggs in the second - whisk them well - and crumbs in the third.

Dredge chilled croquette balls in corn starch, shaking off excess. Arrange on parchment lined baking sheet as you go.

One at a time, dip croquettes into egg, allow excess to drip off, then roll in crumbs. Place crumb covered croquettes back onto parchment lined baking sheet as you finish crumb coating all of the remaining pieces.

Chill dipped croquettes for another 30 minutes.

Heat oil to 350 F (180 C). You can use a deep fryer, or a heavy pan. If not using a deep fryer, use a deep, heavy pot, filled to at least 3" deep.

Once oil reaches temperature, fry croquettes in small batches until nicely browned and crispy. This should take about 2-3 minutes per side. Allow oil to come back up to temperature between batches.

Transfer fried croquettes to paper towel lined sheet to drain, Serve hot.

Mushroom Croquettes

Crawfish Fritters

Crawfish Fritters

The night before this recipe was developed, we were drunkenly watching "True Blood"... and one of the characters brought up "crawfish fritters". I had no idea that was even a thing!

After scolding a few of my southern friends for not having educated me on the existence of this miracle food - I'm a crayfish FIEND - I had to commit the idea to a "to do" list for the next day. As amazing as it sounded as a late night munch, I didn't have any oil for frying.

Having never had them before, I can't actually say how these compare to the real thing. I basically took the idea of it, and designed what I think a crayfish fritter should be. For starters, I wanted the Cajun / Creole "trinity" involved - onions, celery, and peppers. I wanted the same sort of seasoning I do in my Jambalaya, and I wanted a corn based batter, reminiscent of hush puppies. I also wanted a pretty high ratio of "good stuff" to batter.

I buy crayfish tail meat in little 1 lb freezer packs - meat only, no shells. If you can't find crayfish meat, you could substitute chopped cooked shrimp, lobster, or crab.

Makes about 25 fritters

Crayfish tail meat	1 lb	500 g
Rib celery, finely chopped	1	1
Small onion, finely chopped	½	½
Green bell pepper, finely chopped	½	½
Olive oil	1 Tbsp	15 ml
Garlic cloves, pressed or minced	2-3	2-3
Finely chopped green onions	2 Tbsp	30 ml
Masa flour	3/4 cup	175 ml
White rice flour	1/4 cup	50 ml
Baking powder	½ tsp	2 ml
Salt	½ tsp	2 ml
Cayenne	½ tsp	2 ml
Pepper	½ tsp	2 ml
Dried sage	½ tsp	2 ml
Dried thyme	1/4 tsp	1 ml
Dried oregano	pinch	pinch
Large eggs, beaten	3	3
Gluten-free beer or milk	1 cup	250 ml

Vegetable or canola oil for deep frying

If your crayfish meat is frozen, thaw it and drain well. Rinse the tail meat if you like: The fatty liquid surrounding it adds flavour, but some think it adds too much flavour - it can be fishy. Pat dry with paper towels, set aside.

Sauté celery, onion, and bell pepper in olive oil until almost tender. Add garlic, sauté for another minute or so. Remove from heat, stir in crayfish meat and green onions, allow to cool.

Combine flours, baking powder, salt, and seasonings. Add eggs and beer/milk, stir just until combined. Allow to sit for 10 minutes, before stirring in vegetable/meat mix.

Start heating your vegetable oil to 375 F (190 C) – you'll want at least 2-3" of oil in your pot or deep fryer.

Use a small ice cream scoop or two spoons to carefully scoop small amounts (less than 1/4 cup) of batter into the preheated oil. Fry for a few minutes on each side, until fritters are golden brown and cooked through. Use a slotted metal spoon to transfer cooked fritters to paper towels.

Serve hot, with zesty remoulade dip.

Zesty Remoulade Dip

Makes about 1 ½ cups

Mayonnaise	1 cup	250 ml
Dijon Mustard	1/4 cup	50 ml
Prepared horseradish	2 Tbsp	30 ml
Pickle brine or lemon juice	1 Tbsp	15 ml
Finely chopped parsley	2 Tbsp	30 ml
Finely chopped green onions	1 Tbsp	15 ml
Garlic cloves, pressed or minced	2	2
Cayenne	1/4-1/2 tsp	1-2 ml
Paprika	1/4 tsp	1 ml
Salt and pepper		

Combine all ingredients, stirring until smooth. Cover and chill until ready to use - ideally for at least 1 hour.

Soft Pretzels

This recipe is the result of MUCH frustration, trying to get things just right - it's definitely a "holy grail" recipe. When it finally happened, I basically lost my mind all over social media, including posting a barely-coherent video of me repeatedly squishing a piece to show how soft it was. I was in shock - it was SO good!

The only attribute these lack is that the texture isn't the best at room temperature - they really firm up. They're at their best fresh out of the oven, but are also great reheated. You know, much like full-gluten soft pretzels. :)

The missing piece was the protein. High protein gluten-free flours weren't giving me the flavour I wanted, while lower protein flours weren't giving me the texture I wanted. As I was mixing up a protein shake, it hit me - protein powder might come in unflavoured. That MIGHT work. A quick cruise on Amazon found me exactly what I wanted - unflavoured whey protein (Now Foods brand). A few days later it was in my hands, and a few hours later... the aforementioned social media flip-out. This also helped with the development of the bagels in chapter 2!

For additional flavour, you can substitute warm gluten-free beer in place of the water, if desired.

Warm water	1 cup	250 ml
Light brown sugar	2 Tbsp	30 ml
Active dry yeast	2 ½ tsp	22 ml
Light buckwheat flour	3/4 cup	175 ml
White rice flour	3/4 cup	175 ml
Unflavoured whey protein powder	½ cup	125 ml
Potato starch	1/4 cup	50 ml
Sweet rice flour	1/4 cup	50 ml
Xanthan gum	1 tsp	5 ml
Baking powder	½ tsp	2 ml
Salt	½ tsp	2 ml
Vegetable oil	1/4 cup	50 ml
Large egg	1	1
Nonstick spray		
Potato starch	1/3 cup+	75 ml+
Water	3 quarts	3 L
Baking soda	1/4 cup	50 ml
Large egg	1	1
cold water	1 Tbsp	15 ml
Coarse sea salt		

Combine warm water with brown sugar, stir until sugar is almost dissolved. Add yeast, stirring until incorporated. Cover bowl with plastic wrap. Set aside in a warm place for 10 minutes, or until foamy.

In a large bowl, combine flours, protein powder, starch, xanthan gum, baking powder, and salt. Add oil and egg, stirring until well distributed. Pour in yeast mixture, stirring until well combined - it will be VERY wet.

Generously spray a large, clean metal or glass bowl with nonstick spray. Add dough to the bowl, loosely cover with plastic wrap, set aside in a warm spot to rise for an hour or two, until doubled in size.

Once the dough has doubled in size, stir remaining potato starch into the dough. Using lightly greased hands, stir/knead until no longer *super* sticky - it'll be a little sticky. Use a little more potato starch if needed. Return to bowl, loosely cover with plastic wrap, and allow to rise for another 30 minutes.

Divide dough into 4 equal portions. Lightly dust a clean surface with potato starch, roll out dough ball into a longish "snake". Twist into a pretzel shape, pinch cross points to secure. Be gentle when working with the dough - the roll will break easier than full gluten dough does. Allow pretzels to rise for another 30 minutes in a warm place.

Preheat oven to 375 F (190 C). Line a baking sheet with parchment paper, set aside

Bring water to a gentle boil in a large pot. Add baking soda, stir until combined.

Gently transfer the pretzels - one or two at a time - to the pot of water; cook for about a minute on each side. Gently stir as they boil, to ensure that the entire surface of each is in contact with the water at some point. Use a slotted spoon to transfer each pretzel to prepared baking sheet.

Whisk together egg and water, brush this mixture across the tops of the pretzels. Generously sprinkle the tops with coarse sea salt. Bake for about 25 minutes, until golden brown.

Allow to cool for a minute or two before eating, serve with Mustard-Cheddar Dip:

Mustard-Cheddar Dip

Gluten-free beer*	1 cup	250 ml
Mustard of choice	1-2 Tbsp	15-30 ml
Shredded sharp cheddar cheese	12 oz	375 g
Corn starch	2 Tbsp	30 ml
Salt and pepper		

Whisk beer and mustard together in a small saucepan, bring to a simmer over medium heat. In a separate bowl, toss cheese with corn starch.

Add about half of the cheese to the pot, stirring until melted in. Add the rest, continue stirring until everything is melted and smooth. Season with salt and pepper to taste. Serve hot!

* You can use milk or chicken broth in place of beer

Soft Pretzels

Potato Skins

Potato Skins

While potato skins tend to be inherently gluten-free, they also tend to be served in venues that are too ripe for cross contamination to risk it. Sports bars not only don't tend to have dedicated space and equipment for gluten-fee, they share fryers!

So, here's how you make perfect potato skins at home. Aside from the speed and ease of preparing them – no deep frying! – I developed this recipe to make judicious used of bacon – not only the bacon itself, but the drippings. "Waste not, want not", right? Before you ever get to topping these babies with bacon, you've already cooked the potato skins with bacon fat, AND sautéed mushrooms in it. You're welcome! Muahahah!

Serves 2-4 people

Large russet potatoes	4	4
Bacon	1 lb	500 g
Baby bella mushrooms	8 oz	250 g
Nonstick Spray or vegetable oil		
Salt & Pepper		
Shredded Swiss cheese		
Hot sauce or BBQ sauce of choice		
Shredded cheddar cheese		
Sour cream		
Green onions, sliced		

Preheat oven to 450 F (230 C). Use a fork to prick potatoes all over. Place on a microwave safe dish and microwave for 20 minutes on high.

While the potatoes are cooking, chop and fry the bacon until as crispy as you like it. Strain out the bacon and set aside. Reserve 1 tbsp of bacon drippings in the pan, transferring the rest of it to a small heat proof bowl.

Sauté the mushrooms in the pan with 1 Tbsp bacon fat, until soft. Strain off and set aside.

Remove potatoes from microwave. Slice in half and carefully scoop out most of the potato flesh. (Sometimes, we'll add shredded cheddar and sour cream to this, mash it up, and use it as a filling for some of the potato skins… twice baked potato!)

Spray a broiling pan with nonstick spray or brush some vegetable oil to lightly coat. Place potato skins in the pan, cut sides up. Brush generously with remaining melted bacon fat, season with salt and pepper. Roast for 10-12 minutes, flip all skins over, and roast for another 10 minutes.

Remove skins from oven, flip over, and top as you would like. We like to do some with mushrooms and Swiss, and others with hot/BBQ sauce, bacon, and cheddar.

Return pan to the oven, cook until everything is hot and melted. If you'd like some browning, broil it for a couple of minutes on high. Top with sour cream and green onions, serve hot!

Broccoli Cheddar Soup

Main Dishes

Broccoli Cheddar Soup

Not just a thinned out broccoli fondue, this is a well balanced soup. The crunch of the celery - if you don't overcook it - really adds some nice texture and interest to the dish.

If you like your soup a bit thicker, feel free to cut down the amount of chicken broth added.

Makes 6-8 servings

Olive oil	2 Tbsp	30 ml
Ribs celery, thinly sliced	2	2
Medium onion, chopped	1	1
Broccoli florets	3-4 cups	750-1000 ml
Large carrots, grated	2	2
Garlic cloves, pressed or minced	3	3
Salt and pepper		
Butter	1/4 cup	50 ml
White rice flour	1/3 cup	75 ml
Dijon mustard	2 Tbsp	30 ml
Chicken broth	3 cups	750 ml
Gluten-free beer of choice	12 oz	375 ml
Milk	3 cups	750 ml
Shredded sharp Cheddar cheese	6 cups	1500 ml
Shredded Parmesan cheese	1/4 cup	50 ml

In a large pot, combine olive oil, celery, and onion. Cook over medium heat until onions begin to soften. Add broccoli, carrots, and garlic, sprinkle with a little salt and pepper, and cook until vegetables are fairly tender.

Add butter, stir until melted. Sprinkle rice flour over the vegetable and butter mixture, gently stir to combine. Cook - stirring frequently - for 2 minutes.

Once 2 minutes have passed, add Dijon mustard and whisk to combine before adding chicken broth, beer, and milk. Bring soup just up to a simmer, add cheeses and cook, stirring constantly, until cheese is melted and soup is smooth. Season with salt and pepper to taste, serve hot.

Cream of Celery Soup

82

Cream of Celery Soup

This cream of celery soup has an elegant and refined taste for something so simple. The white wine elevates it beyond anything you'd get out of a can, but is optional. (The alcohol does cook off!)

If you would like to use this in place of condensed soup, cut the broth down to 1 cup, and see if you like the texture. Add more broth as necessary.

Makes about 4-6 servings

Celery, trimmed	2 bunches	2 bunches
Small onion	1	1
Olive oil	2 Tbsp	30 ml
Garlic cloves, pressed or minced	2	2
Chicken broth, divided	3 cups	750 ml
Butter	1/4 cup	50 ml
Rice flour	1/4 cup	50 ml
Dry white wine (or chicken broth)	½ cup	125 ml
Heavy whipping cream	1 cup	250 ml
Salt and pepper		

Optional, but makes for a smoother soup: Peel the "strings" off the celery. I like to break each stalk in half, exposing the strings so they are easily peeled off.

Rough chop celery and onion. In a food processor, blitz celery and onion together until very finely chopped. Add to a pan with olive oil, and garlic, cook for 5-10 minutes, until vegetables go soft and translucent. Add 2 cups of broth, cover simmer for 20 minutes.

Transfer soup mixture to a blender, or use a stick blender to puree it. For a smoother soup, you can run this through a wire strainer - we usually don't, though. Return pureed soup to main pot.

In a smaller pot, melt butter. Add rice flour, whisking until smooth. Cook for 2 minutes, whisking frequently. Whisk in wine, until flour mixture is smooth. Add remaining chicken broth, bring just to a boil before simmering for 3 minutes. Add heavy cream, heat just to a simmer - do not allow it to boil.

Stir cream mixture into main pot, stirring well to full combine. Season with salt and pepper, to taste.

Serve hot, or use in the creation of casseroles

Seafood Chowder

Seafood Chowder

When I was living in Newfoundland, I ate the best chowder - literally anywhere I would go! Unlike the delicate clam chowders I'd had before that time, these were loaded with multiple types of fish and shellfish, big chunks of goodness - very hearty. It pretty much wrecked me for clam chowder. So, this isn't the cheapest dish to make, especially for those of us who live inland. It does, however, make a fair amount.. and it's relatively quick and easy to make.

I like to make a flavoured stock for it just before making the chowder - See page 87. If you have fish bones or crab shells, you can use those as well as / instead of the shrimp shells.

Makes 6-8 servings

Boneless cod loins	2 lbs	1 Kg
Boneless salmon fillet	1 lb	500 g
Medium or large shrimp	1 lb	500 g
Bay scallops	½ lb	250 g
Butter	1/4 cup	50 ml
Large onion	1	1
Ribs celery, chopped or sliced	3	3
Large carrot, peeled and sliced	1	1
Large parsnip, peeled and sliced	1	1
Large yellow or red potatoes	4	4
Garlic cloves, pressed or minced	4	4
Seafood, chicken or vegetable stock	8 cups	2 L
Butter	½ cup	125 ml
White rice flour	2/3 cup	150 ml
White wine	1 cup	250 ml
Heavy cream	3 cups	750 ml
Savory (optional), salt and pepper		

Chop cod loins and salmon into bite sized pieces. Add to a large bowl along with shrimp and bay scallops, chill until ready to use.

In a large pot, melt butter. Add onion, celery, carrots, and parsnips to the pot, sauté just until onion and celery soften and go translucent - don't brown them. Chop potatoes into bite sized pieces, add to the pot along with garlic and stock. Bring to a boil, reduce heat slightly and simmer for 10 minutes.

While soup is boiling, make a light roux: In a medium saucepan, melt remaining butter. Add rice flour, whisk until smooth. Cook, stirring constantly, for 1 minute. Add white wine, whisking until smooth. Add heavy cream, once again whisking until smooth. Allow mixture to heat just to steaming.

Add seafood and cream mixture to the main pot, gently stir well to combine. Allow to cook for 5 to 10 minutes - without coming to a boil - or until the seafood is cooked through and chowder has thickened. Season with savoury, salt and pepper to taste, serve hot.

Gumbo

This isn't a super traditional gumbo for two reasons... neither of which relate to the use of flour. No, both are more personal taste and/or sensory issues, for us!

For one, okra. HATE IT. I'm not a picky eater in the slightest, but I can't stand okra. Secondly, I'm not big on the texture that file powder brings to gumbo, so I leave it out. If you like okra, go ahead and add some - just sauté it first, to tone down the nastiness. (Sorry!). If you like file, stir in a couple teaspoons worth after the whole thing is finished cooking. This is a very satisfying meal, great for a cold day. Warms you up!

Olive oil	2 Tbsp	30 ml
Andouille sausage, sliced	1 lb	500 g
Boneless skinless chicken breast	2 lb	1 Kg
Butter	½ cup	125 ml
White rice flour	1 cup	250 ml
Large onion, chopped	1	1
Green bell peppers, chopped	2	2
Ribs celery, chopped	5	5
Garlic cloves, pressed or minced	6	6
Sliced green onions	½ cup	125 ml
Chicken broth *	6 cups	1500 ml
Can diced tomatoes (14.5 oz)	1	1
Cayenne	1 ½ tsp	7 ml
Black pepper	1 tsp	5 ml
Dried oregano	1 tsp	5 ml
Dried sage	1 tsp	5 ml
Dried thyme	½ tsp	2 ml
Bay leaves	3	3
Large shrimp, peeled and deveined	1 lb	500 g
Salt		
Prepared rice, for serving		
Fresh parsley and sliced green onions for garnish		

In a large nonstick pan, heat olive oil. Add sausage and chicken, cook until browned. Remove chicken and sausage from pan, set aside.

Melt butter in pan, scraping up any browned bits from the chicken and sausage. Add rice flour, whisk until smooth. Cook, stirring constantly, until this roux turns a nice mahogany colour.

Add onion, bell pepper, and celery, stir well and cook for 5 minutes. Add garlic, green onions, broth, tomatoes, and spices, stir well.

Simmer for 1 hour on medium-low heat, stirring every 10 minutes or so.

Add shrimp, continue to cook for 3 minutes, or until shrimp is cooked through. Season with salt to taste, remove bay leaves. Serve over rice, topped with parsley and sliced green onions.

* This is even better with flavoured broth. Let me preach for a moment...

You should never pay extra for peeled shrimp! In my not-so-humble-opinion, you should always buy shrimp raw and shell on (Easy peel is fine). Those shells are GOLD in their own right, and absolutely worth the extra few minutes to peel them yourself!

Whenever you work with shrimp, just put the uncooked shells into a freezer baggie and freeze until you need them. Then, when you go to make something that could use shrimp stock - this gumbo, jambalaya, seafood risotto, etc - you'll have them on hand for a quick flavour boost.

Measure chicken stock into a large pot, and toss in your shells, along with a few flavouring ingredients. I usually add a few ribs of celery and some wedges of onion. Bring to a boil, then simmer till it tastes amazing - about 15 minutes. Strain off all the solids and discard them - you'll be left with great tasting shrimp stock.

Gumbo

87

Creamy Creole Soup with Cornmeal Dumplings

I've mentioned before that I get really "If you give a mouse a cookie" about things. Home decor? We went from "Need to tile the bathroom" to "let's tile a subtle Fibonacci sequence into the wall" to ".. and Pi on this other wall!", to... 159 digits of pi tiled into our kitchen back splash. Costuming, cooking, whatever. I'll have a simple idea, and by the time I'm done with it... Yeah.

So, when we were grocery shopping one morning, one of the things on the to-make list for photographing this book was cream of shrimp soup... But then I wanted some kick.

... And then I decided to do it Creole. Oh, that needs a deep dark roux! Also: Now I had to add andouille sausage. Oh, and I was also in the mood for dumplings. Let's go with cornmeal ones!

In the end, this no longer resembled the cream of shrimp soup I had originally intended it to be... But was SO much better!

Makes about 6 servings

Andouille sausage	1 lb	500 g
Olive oil	2 Tbsp	30 ml
Green bell pepper, chopped	1	1
Medium onion, chopped	1	1
Ribs celery, "Star Trekked"	3-4	3-4
Garlic cloves, pressed or minced	4	4
Tomato paste	1/4 cup	50 ml
Chicken or shrimp stock (Page 87)	4 cups	1 L
Cayenne	1/2-1 tsp	2-5 ml
Pepper	2 tsp	10 ml
Dried sage	½ tsp	2 ml
Thyme	1/4 tsp	1 ml
Salt		
Butter	½ cup	125 ml
White rice flour	½ cup	125 ml
Heavy cream	2 cups	500 ml
Light buckwheat flour	2/3 cup	150 ml
Millet flour	1/3 cup	75 ml
Yellow cornmeal	1/3 cup	75 ml
Finely chopped green onions	2 Tbsp	30 ml
Finely chopped parsley	2 Tbsp	30 ml
Tapioca starch	2 tsp	10 ml
Baking Powder	2 tsp	10 ml
Salt	½ tsp	2 ml
Shortening	1/4 cup	50 ml
Milk or buttermilk	3/4 cup	175 ml
Raw shrimp, shelled and deveined	1 lb	500 g

Slice the skin of each andouille sausage, emptying the meat into a large pot. Break it up into bite sized chunks, and drizzle the olive oil over it. Cook over medium high heat until sausage is well browned. Add pepper, onion, and celery to the pot, sauté for 2 minutes or so. Add garlic and tomato paste, continue cooking until tomato paste is browned and fragrant. Add stock and spices, stir well, and turn heat down to low.

In a small pan, melt butter. Add rice flour, whisk until smooth. Cook, stirring constantly, until this roux turns a nice mahogany colour. Slowly and carefully, add heavy cream - it will sputter at first. Whisk mixture as cream gets added, continue whisking until smooth.

Add cream mixture to main pot, stirring to fully incorporate it. Turn heat up to medium and keep at a simmer while you prepare the dumplings:

In a medium sized bowl, mix together flours, cornmeal, green onion, parsley, tapioca starch, baking powder, and salt. Measure shortening into the same bowl, and cut into the dry ingredients using a pastry cutter or fork(s). The idea is to work it in until it's evenly distributed throughout, in very small pieces.

Add milk/buttermilk, stir just until dough comes together. Don't over stir or beat it. If dough is too crumbly, add a small amount of extra milk.

Add shrimp to soup pot, stir gently. Immediately drop rounded tablespoons of dumpling dough into boiling soup. Cover and simmer for 15 minutes WITHOUT LIFTING THE LID.

Serve hot. We like to garnish it with parsley or sliced green onions, but that's entirely optional.

Chicken Pot Pie

This recipe looks like a big undertaking because of the number of ingredients, but actually comes together really quickly - especially if you prepare and lay out all of your ingredients before getting started. I like to use a grocery store rotisserie chicken for this - it's quick, easy, and lends a great flavour to the dish. Be sure to save the skin and carcass to make soup stock!

If you don't feel like roasting the corn, you can skip roasting and just add the raw kernels to the mix - I just find the roasting adds such a great flavour to this dish. If you don't have access to fresh sweet corn, use about 1 cup of frozen corn kernels.

White rice flour	3/4 cup	175 ml
Light buckwheat flour	3/4 cup	175 ml
Millet flour	½ cup	125 ml
Sweet rice flour	1/4 cup	50 ml
Corn starch	1/4 cup	50 ml
Xanthan gum	2 tsp	10 ml
Cream cheese, cut into chunks	8 oz	250 g
Cold butter, cut into chunks	½ cup	125 ml
Large egg	1	1
Cold water	1/3 cup+	75 ml+
Roasted chicken	1	1
Corn, roasted	1 ear	1 ear
Olive oil	1 Tbsp	15 ml
Small onion, chopped	1	1
Carrots, peeled and sliced	2	2
Sliced mushrooms	8 oz	250 g
Ribs celery, "Star Trekked"	2-3	2-3
Garlic cloves, pressed or minced	2	2
Frozen peas	1 cup	250 ml
Butter	1/3 cup	75 ml
White rice flour	½ cup	125 ml
Dry white wine (or chicken broth)	1/4 cup	50 ml
Chicken broth	1 3/4 cups	425 ml
Milk	3/4 cup	175 ml
Dried savoury	1 Tbsp	15 ml
Salt and pepper, to taste		
Large egg	1	1

Measure flours, corn starch, and xanthan gum into the bowl of your food processor, blitz to combine. Add cream cheese, butter, and egg, blitz a few times until mixture resembles gravel. Stream in cold water as you run the food processor, just long enough to start to bring it together as a dough – you may need to use a little more or less water. Do NOT over-process it!

Remove dough from processor, knead lightly to bring it together as a ball. Wrap in plastic film, chill for 1 hour.

Preheat oven to 425 F (220 C)

Strip all of the meat from the chicken, chop into bite sized pieces and set aside. Use a sharp knife to remove kernels from the corn, set aside.

In a large saucepan, combine olive oil, onion, carrots and mushrooms, cook until onion starts to soften and become translucent. Add celery and garlic, sauté for another minute or two. Add corn, peas, and butter; continue cooking until butter is melted.

Sprinkle rice flour over mixture, stir well to combine. Add white wine, stir until well combined. Add chicken broth and milk, stir until liquid mixture is smooth. Add chicken and savoury; season with salt and pepper to taste. Remove from heat.

Divide dough in half, roll your crusts out to about 1/4" thick. Line a deep dish pie pan with one crust, trim the edges of the crust to only slightly longer than the edge of the pie plate.

Spoon filling into prepared crust, cover with the other crust. I like to make a lattice top, but feel free to use a full crust on top - just be sure to cut some slits into it to vent the steam! Use your fingers to crimp/ruffle the edge of the pie. Whisk egg with 1 Tbsp water, brush over crust.

Bake pie for 15 minutes, turn the oven down to 400, bake another 20 minutes, or until crust is golden. Serve hot!

Pelmeni

Pelmeni

Shortly before finding out that I had to go gluten-free, I had pelmeni for the first time. It was at a little local Russian restaurant, and I was in love!

Pelmeni are little Russian meat dumplings that look a bit like Ravioli, depending on how you assemble them. They're boiled in water or broth before being served. Some people like to eat these just on their own, I like them in a broth, with a bunch of fresh dill. The dill really brightens up the whole thing.

This is my gluten-free version. The dough is nice and soft, and doesn't give you attitude. The cooked pelmeni has a great texture - not gummy or overly chewy.

When assembling these, you'll want to make sure to use just enough cornstarch so it'll roll out, but not enough to really dry it out. When you're folding the rounds, it works easier if the underside is a little starchier, and the side facing up is a little more wet - it'll stick to itself better.

Makes about 4-6 servings

Sour cream	1 cup	250 ml
Large eggs	2	2
Warm milk	1/4 cup	50 ml
Vegetable oil	1/4 cup	50 ml
Tapioca starch	2/3 cup	150 ml
Sweet rice flour	1/3 cup	75 ml
Potato starch	1/3 cup	75 ml
Corn starch	1/3 cup	75 ml
Sorghum flour	1 cup	250 ml
Salt	½ tsp	2 ml
Xanthan gum	2 tsp	10 ml

In a food processor or stand mixer, blitz/beat sour cream, eggs, milk, and oil together until well combined.

In a separate bowl, whisk together remaining ingredients until well combined. Add to wet ingredients, blitz/beat until a sticky dough comes together. Wrap dough in plastic film, allow to rest on counter for 45 minutes. While waiting, work on the filling:

Small onion	1	1
Lean ground beef	½ lb	250 g
Ground pork	½ lb	250 g
Salt	½ tsp	2 ml
Pepper	½ tsp	2 ml

Peel and chop onion, puree in food processor or blender until basically liquified. In a large bowl, gently mix beef, pork, onion, salt and pepper.

To assemble:

Potato or corn starch		
Bay leaf	1	1
Salt	2 tsp	10 ml
Melted butter		
Fresh dill, parsley, and/or sliced green onions		

Dust clean work surface generously with potato or corn starch. Roll out dough, aiming to get it pretty thin – 1/16th – 1/8" of an inch or so. When you're first starting out, a bit thicker is ok – you'll just have a bit more dough to bite through to get to your yummy filling!

Cut dough with glass or round cookie cutter – I like to use a glass that's about 2.5" in diameter. Knead excess dough into a ball, roll out again, and repeat until all of the dough is used up.

Place about 1 tsp of filling in the center of each round. Lightly brush the edges with water, which will act as a glue.

Pick a dough round up in your non-dominant hand, and use your good hand to fold the dough around the filling, pressing air out and sealing the edge from one side to the other. Make sure your pelmeni are sealed well, or they will explode when you cook them! Also, I like to flatten them out a little.

Bring the two corners in to touch each other, connecting to form a round dumpling. Repeat for all remaining dough rounds.

Bring a large pot of water to a low boil - too rough of a boil will rip your pelmeni apart! Add bay leaf and salt, stir well. Drop a few pelmeni in at a time – our pot can take about a dozen. Cook until all rise to the surface, then for 5 minutes longer.

Remove cooked pelmeni from water, lightly toss with melted butter. This will prevent them from sticking together. Enjoy as-is, or fry them in butter. Serve with some sour cream (with a sprinkling of dill, parsley, and/or green onions), or in a broth.

Theoretically, you can freeze these (individually on a baking sheet, then bag them together when frozen).. but unless you make several batches, they'll never make it to the freezer!

Sweet Potato Gnocchi

The nice thing about sweet potato gnocchi is that you avoid one of the big problem areas of making traditional gnocchi - boiling potatoes. For sweet potato gnocchi, the sweet potatoes are dry cooked, not boiled - so heavy, doughy, waterlogged dumplings aren't likely to happen!

As with traditional gnocchi though, you'll want to handle every stage of mixing with a light hand - keep it as fluffy and loose as possible up to the point of rolling. Handling everything gently will ensure that you'll end up with soft, pillowy gnocchi.

When deciding how I wanted to serve this, I immediately thought of the brown butter sage sauce that my friend Matt made for me at one point. His was on a ricotta and lemon ravioli, but just thinking of those crispy bits of sage.. yeah, I wanted something like that for this. Also, mushrooms. LOVE mushrooms.

A note: you're looking for tubers that have orange flesh, and a lot of the time, they're sold as "yams" (and those aren't necessarily even yams!). "Yam gnocchi" sounds weird though... so, we'll call it "Sweet potato", though you may have to buy something labeled as "yams". Isn't a lack of consistency in terminology FUN?

The texture is great - actual gnocchi. No gumminess or sandyness, they were easy to work with and held together well. If you're like us, you'll want to double the mushrooms in the sauce - they are FABULOUS in this.

Makes 4 servings

Large yams / sweet potatoes	2	2
White rice flour	1 cup	250 ml
Potato starch	3/4 cup	175 ml
Sweet rice flour	½ cup	125 ml
Millet flour	1/4 cup	50 ml
Salt	1 1/4 tsp	6 ml
Xanthan gum	½ tsp	2 ml
Ground nutmeg (optional)	pinch	pinch
Large eggs, beaten	3	3
Potato starch for rolling		
Salt		

Scrub and pat the sweet potatoes dry, use a fork to pierce each of them all over. Cook them in one of two ways:

1. Roast at 350 for 45-50 minutes, or until soft.
2. Place in a microwave safe baking dish, nuke for 25 minutes or so, until soft.

Either way, place cooked sweet potatoes aside and allow to cool a bit before proceeding.

Once potatoes are cool enough to handle, peel skin off them and puree or put through a ricer - make sure there are no lumps. Measure out 2 cups of sweet potato, reserving the rest for a future use (can be frozen.). Allow to cool completely before proceeding.

In a separate bowl, whisk together flours, starch, salt, xanthan gum, and nutmeg to combine well. Add flour mixture to cooled sweet potato, gently fold to combine. Add eggs, once again gently folding to combine. Cover tightly with plastic film, Chill for 1 hour.

Generously dust your work surface with potato starch. Dump gnocchi dough out, knead gently to bring together into a soft ball. If the dough is sticky, add a little potato starch until it's workable.

Divide dough into 8-10 roughly equal pieces. One at a time, roll each out into long "snakes", each about the thickness of a thumb. Cut each roll into bite-sized pieces, about 3/4"- 1" long.

If you're feeling lazy, you can cook these up as-is. Otherwise, you can roll them over a fork to produce the traditional ridged gnocchi shape. There are many possible ways to do this, and you may want to play with it a bit until you find your own groove. For me, I gently (but firmly!) roll each gnocchi over the back of the fork, aiming towards the pointed ends of the tines. As I roll, the gnocchi will curl over itself into a slight "c" shape. Practice, experiment, and if necessary - Youtube has great tutorials for a variety of methods.

Start a fresh pot of boiling water, and salt it well. Bring it to a gentle, not rolling boil, and cook your gnocchi in batches. As they float to the top, allow them to cook another minute or so before using a slotted spoon to remove them, transferring to a clean bowl or plate.

Serve hot and fresh, with sauce of your choice. As shown:

Brown Butter Sauce with Mushrooms and Sage

Olive oil	1 Tbsp	15 ml
Small onion, thinly sliced	1	1
Baby bella mushrooms, sliced	8 oz	250 g
Salt and pepper		
Garlic cloves, pressed	3	3
Butter	1 cup	250 ml
Fresh sage leaves, packed & chopped	1/4 cup	50 ml
Fresh lemon juice	2 tsp	10 ml

Heat olive oil in a nonstick pan. Sauté onion and mushrooms until they start to soften, seasoning with a little salt and pepper.

Add garlic, butter, sage leaves, and lemon juice. Cook for a few minutes, until butter starts to brown and sage leaves crisp up. Add gnocchi to pan, toss to coat.

Serve hot.

Sweet Potato Gnocchi

Tuna Casserole

Tuna Casserole

Tuna casserole - to most people - is a quick and easy thing to make, given the widely available condensed cream of soup options. With much fewer options for those who are gluten-free, I decided to make a from-scratch version. ... but if I'm going to the effort, it's going to be dressed up slightly. Fresh ingredients make for a nicer, refined flavour... So why not add a bit of wine?

This casserole is nice and rich, with distinct flavours apparent. It's definitely a departure from the uniform flavour blanket that canned soup gives! Even if you're not a tuna fan, the albacore tuna doesn't scream "canned tuna" - my husband is not a fan of fishy fish, but will down a bowl of this in no time.

Note: I find brown rice pasta to be the best tasting, and best to work with.

Makes 6 servings.

Dry gluten-free pasta of choice	16 oz	500 g
Small onion	1	1
Ribs celery	6	6
Olive oil	2 Tbsp	30 ml
White mushroom slices	8 oz	250 g
Garlic cloves, pressed or minced	2	2
Butter	1/4 cup	50 ml
White rice flour	1/4 cup	50 ml
Dry white wine (or chicken broth)	½ cup	125 ml
Chicken broth	1 ½ cup	
Heavy whipping cream	1 cup	250 ml
Shredded Parmesan cheese, divided	1 ½ cups	375 ml
Frozen peas	1 cup	250 ml
Cans solid white albacore tuna	2 small	2 small
Salt and pepper		
Crushed plain potato chips	1 cup	250 ml

Preheat oven to 400 F (200 C). Cook noodles just to al dente, drain and set aside when done. While cooking the noodles:

In a food processor, blitz celery and onion together until very finely chopped. Add to a large saucepan along with olive oil, mushrooms, and garlic. Cook for 5-10 minutes, until vegetables go soft and onions/celery are translucent.

Add butter, allow to fully melt, then whisk in rice flour. Add wine, whisking until flour mixture is smooth. Add chicken broth, bring just to a boil before simmering for 5 minutes. Add heavy cream, heat just to a simmer - do not allow it to boil.

Stir in half of the Parmesan, and the frozen peas. Drain tuna, add to pot along with noodles. Season with salt and pepper, to taste. Transfer to a 9" round baking dish, top with remaining Parmesan and crushed chips. Bake for 15 minutes, serve hot.

Pasta Primavera

Pasta Primavera

Pasta primavera is all about contrasts - contrast in texture between the noodles and crunchy vegetables. Contrast in mouthfeel between the bright freshness of those vegetables, and the richness of a butter, cream, and cheese based sauce. Also, visual contrast when it comes to the colours of the vegetables, and those of the pasta and sauce.

My husband said "It's like a bowl of spring"... Fitting, as the name literally means "spring pasta"! It reminds him of going to the farmers market, getting a bunch of in season vegetables, coming home and having me make something "magical" with them - his words. I married well!

Serves 4-6

Dry gluten-free pasta, like penne	1 lb	500 g
Butter	2 Tbsp	30 ml
Corn starch	2 tsp	10 ml
Garlic cloves, minced or pressed	2	2
Heavy cream	2 cups	500 ml
Grated Asiago or Parmesan cheese	½ cup	125 ml
Fresh basil leaves, chiffonade	1-2 Tbsp	15-30 ml
Salt and pepper		
Olive Oil	1 Tbsp	15 ml
White onion, thinly sliced	1	1
Garlic cloves, pressed or minced	2	2
Red onion, sliced	½	½
Small yellow squash, sliced	1	1
White mushrooms, sliced	4 oz	125 g
Small broccoli florets	1 cup	250 ml
Green pea pods	1 cup	250 ml
Green onion, thinly sliced	1	1
Carrots, thinly sliced	2	2
Red bell pepper, sliced	1	1

In a large pot, bring water to a boil. Cook pasta per directions. While pasta is cooking, prepare sauce and vegetables:

In a medium sauce pan, melt butter. Add cornstarch, whisk until smooth. Add garlic, whisk until well combined. Add heavy cream, bring JUST to a boil. Add cheese, continue stirring until melted and smooth. Add basil, reduce heat to low. Season with salt and pepper to taste.

In a large fry pan or wok, sauté onion and garlic in olive oil until onion goes translucent. Add rest of vegetables, sauté JUST until warm. You don't want them to actually cook through or go soft.

Strain pasta, gently toss with sauce and vegetables, serve immediately.

Pineapple Fried Rice

Pineapple Fried Rice

This is our favourite fried rice recipe - the seafood and pineapple go so well together, and the mix of flavours and textures just really hits the spot.

As with all fried rice, the key is to use prepared rice that is at least a day old, and chilled. Using freshly prepared rice leads to weird textures, and mushy rice.

Makes about 4 servings

Large eggs, beaten	2	2
Olive oil, divided	2 Tbsp	30 ml
Salt, pepper		
Gluten-free soy sauce	2 Tbsp	30 ml
Fish sauce	1 Tbsp	15 ml
Lime juice	1 Tbsp	15 ml
Sesame oil	2 tsp	10 ml
Ginger paste	2 tsp	10 ml
Sriracha sauce	1-2 tsp+	5-10 ml+
Garlic cloves, pressed or minced	2-3	2-3
Can of pineapple tidbits, drained	20 oz	567 g
Large red pepper, diced	1	1
Prepared jasmine rice, chilled	4 cups	100 ml
Raw seafood: shrimp and/or scallops	1 lb	500 g
Bean sprouts	1 cup	250 ml
Green onions, thinly sliced	4	4
Unsalted, roasted cashews	½ cup	125 ml
Lime slices for garnish		

Scramble eggs in 1 Tbsp of the olive oil, seasoning with a little salt and pepper, to taste. Remove from heat, chop. Set aside.

Whisk together soy sauce, fish sauce, lime juice, sesame oil, ginger paste, sriracha, and garlic, set aside.

In a large nonstick pan or wok, sauté pineapple and red pepper in remaining olive oil for 5 minutes or so, until pineapple is nicely caramelized. Add chilled rice and soy sauce mixture, stir well to combine. Cook for another 2-3 minutes, or until rice is heated through.

Add seafood, stir well to combine. Continue to cook until seafood is almost cooked through.

Add bean sprouts, green onions, cashews, and scrambled egg, fold gently to combine. Cook until everything is heated through.

Season with salt and pepper, to taste. Serve hot, with lime slices

Hybrid Tacos

Hybrid Tacos

Even before having to go gluten-free, I preferred the flavour of corn tortillas to flour tortillas... but hated the texture. I found the corn ones rough and too prone to cracking. How great would it be to do a hybrid, with all the flavour of a corn tortilla, but that looked and felt like a "flour" tortilla?

The problem: The higher the percentage of non-corn ingredients in the mix, the less it tastes like corn.

Enter my crazy idea: making a "flour" from freeze dried corn! Freeze dried corn is sold as a snack food, but when you run through a food processor, it makes a powder that packs a LOT of flavour. While these look and act like a flour tortilla, I find that they taste even more like corn, than normal corn tortillas. Fresh off the griddle, they taste like roasted sweet corn!

These tortillas stay soft even when cooled, and go really well with any kind of taco fillings.

Makes 6-8 8" tortillas

Masa flour	½ cup	125 ml
Freeze dried corn powder	½ cup	125 ml
Sorghum flour	½ cup	125 ml
Sweet rice flour	1/4 cup	50 ml
Tapioca starch	1/4 cup	50 ml
Xanthan gum	2 tsp	10 ml
Salt	3/4 tsp	3 ml
Baking powder	½ tsp	2 ml
Shortening or lard	1/4 cup	50 ml
Cold water	1 cup	250 ml
Corn starch for rolling		

In a large bowl, whisk together dry ingredients until very well incorporated.

Add shortening/lard to the bowl. Use a potato masher or pastry knife to cut the shortening down to small, irregular pieces - mix should look sort of like gravel.

Add water, stir until well mixed. Knead a few times, just to bring it together - don't over work it! Wrap in dough in plastic film, allow to rest on your counter for 30 minutes.

Generously sprinkle clean work surface with corn starch. Separate dough into 4 equal sized chunks.

One chunk at a time, roll dough out as thin as possible, sprinkling more corn starch as necessary. Cut an 8" round - I like to use a plate or cake pan as a guide - set aside. Collect cuttings from each round, knead together. Repeat rolling and cutting until all the dough is cut into circles.

Cook for 2-3 minutes each side on a smoking hot skillet. Cover freshly cooked tortillas with a towel, repeating until all tortillas are cooked.

Serve right away, or store in an airtight container for a day or two. For best flavour, reheat before use.

Shrimp Tacos

Slaw:

Packet of broccoli slaw	10 oz	300 g
Small purple cabbage, shredded	½	½
Green onions, thinly sliced	3-4	3-4
Cilantro, chopped	2 Tbsp	30 ml
Sour cream	½ cup	125 ml
Lime juice	2 tsp	10 ml
Lime, zest of	1	1
Jalapeno peppers, finely chopped	1-2	1-2
Garlic cloves, pressed or minced	2	2
Salt and pepper		

In a large bowl, combine broccoli slaw, shredded cabbage, green onions, and cilantro, set aside.

In a separate bowl, whisk together remaining ingredients until smooth and well combined. Add to large bowl, stir well to combine. Cover and chill until ready to use.

Grilled Cilantro-Lime Shrimp:

Fresh lime juice	1/4 cup	50 ml
Lime, zest of	1	1
Olive oil	2 Tbsp	30 ml
Garlic cloves, pressed or minced	2	2
Small jalapeno pepper	1	1
Finely chopped cilantro	2 Tbsp	30 ml
Salt and pepper		
Large shrimp, peeled and deveined	1 lb	500 g

In a large bowl, whisk together everything except salt, pepper, and shrimp. Season with salt and pepper to taste. Add shrimp, stir to coat well. Cover and chill for about 30 minutes, then grill shrimp until cooked through.

To serve:

Assemble tacos with grilled marinated shrimp, slaw, sliced mangos, and avocado slices.

Chicken Shahi Korma

Chicken Shahi Korma is our absolute favorite thing to order at our favorite Indian restaurant locally. I mean, to the point where I've never actually ordered a different entree there – I fell in love with it, and don't tend to stray! While we're always in the mood for some Shahi Korma, we're usually far less likely to be in the mood to deal with traffic, noise, and… well, people.

So, a few years ago, I decided to unleash my "Aspie superpower" on this dish - which is inherently gluten-free. You see, if I taste something, I can usually replicate it pretty easily – in terms of end product. In doing this, I don't tend to research the history, techniques, etc – I like to figure most of it out on my own. As a result, there's a good chance that something in my technique and/or ingredients are way off from tradition. I just find that "flying blind" tends to facilitate a more accurate final result.

This recipe may look intimidating, but try to see past the ridiculous ingredient list: it's actually very, very easy to make. Also, all of those spices come together to create a meal that is very much worth the effort!

Makes 6-8 servings

Ingredient	Imperial	Metric
Boneless chicken thighs and or/breast	4 lbs	2 Kg
Lemon juice	3 Tbsp	45 ml
Olive oil	2 Tbsp	30 ml
Salt	½ tsp	2 ml
Pepper	1 tsp	5 ml
Onions, finely chopped	2	2
Ginger paste	2 Tbsp	30 ml
Garlic cloves, pressed or minced	8	8
Cashew butter	½ cup	125 ml
Cardamom pods	5	5
Whole cloves	4	4
Fennel seeds	1 tsp	5 ml
Granulated sugar	1 Tbsp	15 ml
Hot pepper flakes	1 Tbsp	15 ml
Garam masala	2 tsp	10 ml
Ground cinnamon	1 tsp	5 ml
Ground coriander	1 tsp	5 ml
Turmeric	1 tsp	5 ml
Cumin	½ tsp	5 ml
Ground cardamom	½ tsp	5 ml
Chicken broth	1 cup	250 ml
Olive oil	1/4 cup	50 ml
Olive oil	1 Tbsp	15 ml
Tomato paste	3 Tbsp	45 ml
Coconut milk* (Or heavy cream)	2 cups	500 ml
Plain yogurt	1 cup	250 ml

Paneer, cubed	12 oz	375 g
Golden raisins	3/4 cup	175 ml
Cashews	½ -3/4 cup	125-175 ml
Chopped fresh parsley	1/4 cup	50 ml
Chopped fresh cilantro	1/4 cup	50 ml

Cut chicken into large cubes, place in a large bowl. Sprinkle with lemon juice, olive oil, salt, and pepper, toss to coat. Cover, and chill for a few hours or overnight.

Put onions, ginger, garlic, and cashew butter into a blender or food processor – process till it's a thick paste.

Grind cardamom pods, cloves, and fennel seeds with a spice mill or mortar/pestle. Once well ground, add to blender along with sugar, remaining spices, chicken broth and 1/4 cup olive oil, process until smooth.

In a large pan, brown chicken pieces in remaining 1 Tbsp olive oil. As chicken starts to brown, add tomato paste, cook until tomato paste starts to brown and gets very aromatic. Add chicken broth/spice mixture, along with coconut milk/heavy cream and yogurt. Stir well, reduce heat to low, simmer for about 1 hour.

When sauce has thickened, add paneer, raisins, cashews, parsley and cilantro. Stir well, continue to cook for another 15 minutes.

Serve over rice.

* By "coconut milk", I am referring to the thick, creamy type – NOT the watery juice type, and not "coconut creme". This is readily available in the Asian section of major grocers, or in many ethnic grocery shops.

Chicken Shahi Korma

Cod Au Gratin

Cod Au Gratin

Cod au gratin isn't something I was raised on, but a dish I was exposed to while living in Newfoundland - it's VERY popular there, with many people and restaurants all having their own take on it. It's a highly customizable dish!

Cheddar is traditional, but you can use white cheddar, havarti, or any other mild cheese. Gluten-free beer can be substituted for the wine (this is especially good with cheddar). You can leave the savoury out, or substitute parsley, chives, or any other herb you enjoy with mild fish. Sometimes, I'll add chopped up asparagus or broccoli, just to convince myself that it's healthy!

Makes 4-6 servings

Boneless cod loins*	2 lbs	1 Kg
Butter	1/4 cup	50 ml
Small onion, finely chopped	½	½
Garlic cloves, pressed or minced	1-2	1-2
Potato starch	1/4 cup	50 ml
Prepared Dijon mustard	1 Tbsp	15 ml
Dry white wine	1/4 cup	50 ml
Milk	2 1/4 cups	550 ml
Shredded Parmesan cheese	2/3 cup	150 ml
Shredded provolone cheese	1 cup	250 ml
Dried savoury	2 tsp	10 ml
Salt		
Pepper		
Plain potato chips, crumbled	Small bag	Small bag

Preheat oven to 350 F (180 C). Cut cod into 1" pieces, arrange in an 8x8" baking pan. Alternately, you can divide them between 4-6 individual ramekins. Set aside.

In a medium sauce pan, melt butter. Add onion and garlic and cook - stirring frequently - until onions are tender and translucent. Add potato starch to the pot, cook for another minute, stirring frequently. Add Dijon, whisking until well incorporated. Carefully add wine to pot, whisking until smooth. Cook for 2 minutes, whisking frequently.

Add milk, once again whisking until smooth. Heat until mixture starts to thicken. Once sauce mixture starts to thicken, add half of the Parmesan and a small handful of the provolone, stirring until thick, melted, and smooth. Add savoury, season with salt and pepper, to taste.

Pour sauce over fish, stirring to coat and distribute evenly. Scatter provolone cheese across the top of the fish mixture, then remaining parmesan. Spread crumbled potato chips on top. Bake – uncovered- for about 35 (individual ramekins) - 50 minutes (8x8 pan), or until fish is cooked through, and sauce is bubbly. Serve hot.

* If using frozen fish, partially thaw it, cut it, then allow it to fully thaw and DRAIN before putting it in the baking pan.

Asian Inspired Shrimp Cakes

Asian Inspired Shrimp Cakes

This recipe came as a result of a craving for gyoza, combined with a laziness that wasn't conducive to arsing around with making the dough and folding dumplings. These feature all of the flavour, with a fraction of the effort - they whip up in just minutes! These cakes have a great contrast of flavours and textures which all work so well together, especially with a squeeze of lime juice and drizzle of the mayo sauce. Be sure to make the sauce a few hours ahead of time, to give the flavours time to mix.

Makes 2-3 servings as a meal, or 4 servings as an appetizer

Mayonnaise	½ cup	125 ml
Gluten-free soy sauce	1 tsp	5 ml
Rice vinegar	1 tsp	5 ml
Hot pepper flakes	1/4- ½ tsp	1-2 ml
Finely shredded napa cabbage	1 cup	250 ml
Salt	½ tsp	2 ml
Mayonnaise	1/3 cup	75 ml
White rice flour	½ cup	125 ml
Grated ginger	1 tsp	5 ml
Garlic cloves, pressed or minced	1-2	1-2
Green onions, finely chopped	2	2
Toasted sesame seeds	2 Tbsp	30 ml
Sesame oil	2 tsp	10 ml
Large eggs, beaten	2	2
Raw shrimp, peeled and deveined	1 lb	500 g
Fresno chili, finely chopped	1	1
Vegetable oil		
Lime, sliced into wedges	1	1

In a small bowl, combine mayo, soy sauce, vinegar, and pepper flakes, mix until smooth. Cover and chill until use - this is your mayo sauce.

In a large mixing bowl, combine cabbage and salt, stirring to evenly distribute the salt. Allow to sit for 10-15 minutes - this will draw the moisture out of the cabbage. Once time is up, squeeze as much water out of the cabbage as you can, discarding the water. Place the squeezed cabbage back into the mixing bowl.

Add mayo, rice flour, ginger, garlic, green onions, sesame seeds, sesame oil, and beaten eggs to the mixing bowl, stir well to combine. Peel and devein shrimp, finely chop. Add to the mixing bowl along with chili pepper, stir to combine. Cover bowl with plastic and chill for 1 hour.

In a large fry pan, heat 1-2 Tbsp oil over medium heat. In batches, gently drop mixture into back by ½ cup measure, flattening and rounding a little as you go. Be careful not to burn yourself - oil may spatter. Pan fry shrimp cakes until golden brown and cooked through - about 3-4 minutes on each side. Serve warm, with mayo sauce and lime wedges

Chicken Satay

Chicken Satay

Chicken Satay is one of those dishes that is SO close to being gluten-free... but isn't. The soy sauce included in both marinade and dipping sauce renders restaurant satay inedible to most with gluten issues. So, if you've got to make it at home, best to start with an amazing recipe!

The sauce can be made ahead, or as you're grilling the chicken. I like to serve the sauce hot, but it can also be served cool- you'll just want to thin it with a little chicken stock, as it thickens.

Serves 2-4 people

2 lbs boneless skinless chicken breast

Marinade:

Coconut milk	1 cup	250 ml
Olive oil	2 Tbsp	30 ml
Gluten-free soy sauce	1 Tbsp	15 ml
Lime juice	1 Tbsp	15 ml
Light brown sugar	1 Tbsp	15 ml
Garlic cloves, pressed or minced	2	2
Curry powder	1 tsp	5 ml
Salt and pepper		

Sauce:

Coconut milk	1 cup	250 ml
Peanut butter	½ cup	125 ml
Chicken stock	½ cup	125 ml
Lime juice	1 Tbsp	15 ml
Light brown sugar	2 Tbsp	30 ml
Curry powder	2 tsp	10 ml
Gluten-free soy sauce	2 tsp	10 ml
Fish sauce	1 tsp	5 ml
Pepper flakes	1 tsp	5 ml
Garlic clove, pressed or minced	1	1

Cut chicken breasts into relatively uniform strips, about 1.5" across. Place in a bowl for marinating (Ideally with a lid), set aside.

Whisk together all marinade ingredients except salt and pepper, then season with salt and pepper to taste. Pour marinade over chicken strips, gently turning to coat well. Cover and refrigerate for at least 5 hours.

In a medium saucepan, whisk together all sauce ingredients. Bring just to a boil, turn heat down, and simmer for 5 minutes.

Soak wooden skewers in hot water for 30 minutes, before threading with chicken strips. Spray grill with nonstick spray, grill until cooked through- juices should run clear. Serve hot.

Boneless Wings

Boneless Wings

While regular wings tend to be gluten free (always ask first, though, to be sure!)... sometimes you don't want the hassle of eating off the bone, and could really just go for a plate of boneless wings. I have you covered!

The flavour of these boneless "wings" stands well on its own, but is even better when tossed in any of a number of wing sauces - I'm including recipes for a few of my favourites.

We love how the crust on these is absorbent enough to take in the sauce, but still had the crispy, crunchy texture we expect from boneless wings - so it's not like eating a soggy sponge. This recipe ruined us both for the wings we used to get from a major chain restaurant - and my husband isn't even gluten-free!

Boneless, skinless chicken breasts	2 lbs	1 Kg
Salt, pepper		
Cornstarch	3/4 cup	175 ml
Millet flour	½ cup	125 ml
White rice flour	1/4 cup	50 ml
Baking powder	1 tsp	5 ml
Pepper	1 tsp	5 ml
Salt	1 tsp	5 ml
Paprika	½ tsp	2 ml
Garlic powder	½ tsp	2 ml
Cayenne powder	½ tsp	2 ml
Mustard powder	1/4 tsp	1 ml
Onion powder	1/4 tsp	1 ml
Large eggs	3	3
Milk	½ cup	125 ml

Cut chicken breasts into 1" chunks. Season with salt and pepper, set in fridge to rest while you prepare the flour and egg mixtures.

In a large bowl, combine cornstarch, flours, baking powder, and spices, set aside. In a separate bowl, whisk together eggs and milk until smooth.

Lightly dredge all rested chicken in flour mixture, shaking excess flour mixture back into the bowl.

One piece at a time, dip chicken into egg mixture, allow excess liquid to drip off, then roll into flour mixture. Press flour mixture firmly against the chicken to adhere, arrange on a baking sheet. Once all chicken has been dipped and coated, allow to rest in fridge for 15 minutes.

Heat oil 375 F (190 C) - You can use a deep fryer, or a heavy pan. If not using a deep fryer, use a deep, heavy pot, filled to at least 3" deep.

Once oil reaches temperature, fry chicken in batches until nicely browned and crispy. This should take about 5 minutes per batch. Allow oil to come back up to temperature between batches.

Toss Boneless wings with sauce of choice, serve hot.

For oven baked boneless wings:

Heat oven to 400 F (200 C)

Line a large baking sheet with parchment paper, spray with pan spray. Arrange battered and chilled chicken pieces on the pan. Spray chicken with pan spray.

Bake for 20 minutes, flip chicken pieces. Spray once again with pan spray, bake for another 15 minutes, or until cooked through and juices run clear.

Buffalo Sauce

Hot sauce (Like Frank's)	3/4 cup	175 ml
Butter	½ cup	125 ml
Worcestershire or steak sauce	1 tsp	5 ml
Granulated sugar	½ tsp	2 ml
Garlic powder	1/4 tsp	1 ml

Mix ingredients together in saucepan over medium heat, stirring until butter is melted and everything smooth.

Remove sauce from stove, use warm - can be chilled until use and reheated.

Spicy Garlic Sauce

Hot Sauce (Like Frank's)	½ cup	125 ml
Butter, melted	½ cup	125 ml
Chicken broth	3/4 cup	175 ml
Corn starch	1 Tbsp	15 ml
Sugar	2 tsp	10 ml
Garlic powder	1 ½ tsp	7 ml
Pepper, to taste		

Whisk ingredients together in saucepan. Cook over medium heat, stirring until sauce is smooth and has thickened. Use warm - can be reheated.

Jerk Sauce

Small red onion	½	½
Green onion	1	1
Garlic cloves, pressed or minced	4	4
Habanero peppers	2-3	2-3
Gluten-free soy sauce	1/4 cup	50 ml
Orange juice	1/4 cup	50 ml
White vinegar	1/4 cup	50 ml
Packed brown sugar	1/4 cup	50 ml
Olive oil	2 Tbsp	30 ml
Molasses	2 Tbsp	30 ml
Ginger paste	1 Tbsp	30 ml
Fresh thyme leaves	1 Tbsp	30 ml
Allspice	1 tsp	5 ml
Coarse ground black pepper	1 tsp	5 ml
Nutmeg	½ tsp	2 ml
Cinnamon	½ tsp	2 ml
Salt	½ tsp	2 ml
Ground cloves	1/4 tsp	1 ml
Lime, juice of	1	1

Rough chop onion, green onion, garlic, and habaneros, add to a blender or food processor with all other ingredients. Blitz until well processed and smooth.

Transfer mixture to saucepan. Bring to a simmer over medium heat, simmer 5 minutes or so, whisking often. Remove sauce from stove, use warm - can be chilled until use and reheated.

Sweet and Spicy Asian Sauce

Gluten-free soy sauce	1/4 cup	50 ml
Sriracha sauce	1/4 cup	50 ml
Honey	1/4 cup	50 ml
Water or chicken broth	1/4 cup	50 ml
Brown sugar	1/4 cup	50 ml
Rice vinegar	2 Tbsp	30 ml
Garlic cloves, pressed or minced	3	3
Ginger puree	1-2 tsp	5-10 ml
Freshly grated orange zest	1 tsp	5 ml
Corn starch	2 tsp	10 ml
Hot pepper flakes	1/2-1 tsp	2-5 ml

Whisk ingredients together in saucepan. Simmer over medium heat for 5 minutes, stirring until sauce is smooth and thickened. Use warm - can be reheated.

Roasted Garlic Parmesan Sauce

Garlic bulbs	4	4
Olive oil	1 Tbsp	15 ml
Chicken stock	½ cup	125 ml
Butter, melted	1/4 cup	50 ml
Vinegar	2 Tbsp	30 ml
Granulated sugar	1 tsp	5 ml
Corn starch	1 tsp	5 ml
Onion powder	½ tsp	2 ml
Dried thyme	1/4 tsp	1 ml
Dried oregano	1/4 tsp	1 ml
Dried basil	1/4 tsp	1 ml
Hot pepper flakes, optional	1/4-1/2 tsp	1-2 ml
Shredded Parmesan cheese	1 cup	250 ml
Mayonnaise	½ cup	125 ml
Salt and pepper		

Preheat oven to 400 F (200 C). Line a baking sheet with a large piece of aluminum foil.

Peel the outer layers of skin from each of the garlic bulbs. Use a sharp knife to cut about ½" off the pointed top of each bulb. You want to cut enough off that the tops of most cloves of garlic are exposed. Arrange on foil, drizzle with olive oil. Pull sides of foil up and over the garlic to create a sealed "package". Roast for about 40 minutes, or until garlic is golden and soft. Remove from heat, allow to cool to room temperature.

Once cooled, squeeze or spoon actual garlic bulbs into a saucepan, discarding papery skins. Mash lightly. Add remaining ingredients, aside from cheese, mayo, salt, and pepper. Bring to a simmer over medium heat, whisking until smooth. Add cheese, continue stirring until melted and smooth.

Remove sauce from stove, stir in mayonnaise. Season with salt and pepper to taste. Use warm - can be reheated.

Honey Mustard Glaze

Dijon mustard	½ cup	125 ml
Honey	½ cup	125 ml
Butter	1/4 cup	50 ml
Vinegar	2 Tbsp	30 ml
Turmeric	½ tsp	2 ml
Salt and pepper		

Whisk ingredients together in saucepan. Simmer over medium heat for 5 minutes, stirring until sauce is smooth. Season with salt and pepper, to taste. Use warm - can be reheated.

Coconut Shrimp with Spicy Ginger-Orange Sauce

While at a trade show - promoting the first Beyond Flour - I was approached by a man who said that what he REALLY missed was coconut shrimp. It sounded SO good at the time, we decided to work up a recipe that very week.

This recipe comes together quickly, easily, and tastes GREAT! As I'd been demonstrating Sesame chicken that weekend, I was right in the mood for ginger and spicy, while talking to people about my Spicy Orange Chicken had me craving something like that. I decided to combine the two cravings and come up with something to scratch both itches - Spicy Ginger-Orange Sauce. We like to use a lot of ginger, and go with 1 Tbsp... but you can use as little as 1 tsp if you want.

Butterflying the shrimp provides more surface area for the batter, but is not necessary. If you like a higher shrimp-to-batter ratio, feel free to use the shrimp as-is

Makes 4 servings

Medium/large shrimp: peeled, tail on	2 lbs	1 Kg
Salt and pepper		
Garbanzo bean flour	½ cup	125 ml
Corn starch	1/4 cup	50 ml
White rice flour	1/4 cup	50 ml
Baking powder	1 tsp	5 ml
Salt	1 tsp	5 ml
Large eggs	2	2
Gluten-free beer (or chicken broth)	1 cup	250 ml
Garbanzo bean flour	1 cup	250 ml
Unsweetened coconut flakes	3 cups	750 ml
Oil for deep frying – we used vegetable oil		

If you'd like to butterfly your shrimp: use a sharp knife to cut along the back (outside) of the shrimp from end to tail. Be careful to not cut all of the way through! Spread the sides of the shrimp, press gently to flatten.

Butterflied or not, season shrimp with a little salt and pepper, tossing to coat. Set aside.

In a large bowl, combine flours, corn starch, baking powder, and salt. Add eggs and beer/broth, whisk to form a medium-thick batter. All batter to sit for 5-10 minutes, to soften the bean and rice flours.

Place remaining bean flour in a separate bowl, and the coconut in a third bowl.

Dredge shrimp in reserved garbanzo flour, shake off any excess flour, then dredge in rested batter. Allow excess batter to drip off before rolling shrimp in coconut.

Place prepared shrimp on a baking sheet, repeat battering steps with remaining shrimp. Once all shrimp is battered, chill for 15 minutes.

Start heating your oil to 350 F (180 C) – you'll want at least 2-3" of oil in your pot or deep fryer.

Carefully transfer chilled shrimp to the preheated oil, cooking in batches. Fry for 1-2 minutes on each side, until golden brown and cooked all the way through. Use a slotted metal spoon to transfer fried shrimp to paper towels. Serve hot!

Spicy Ginger-Orange Sauce

Orange marmalade	½ cup	125 ml
Honey	1/4 cup	50 ml
Grated ginger	1-3 tsp	5-15 ml
Salt	pinch	pinch
Crushed pepper flakes	1 tsp	5 ml

Whisk together all ingredients in a small saucepan, until smooth. Bring mixture just to a boil, reduce heat and simmer for two minutes. Remove from heat, serve warm or cool.

Coconut Shrimp with Spicy Ginger-Orange Sauce

123

Chewy Lemon Cookies

Desserts

Chewy Lemon Cookies

These are a great go-to cookie to go with tea. Great texture - Soft, slightly chewy - with the brightness of lemon. They aren't overly sweet, not overly intense, just a nicely balanced cookie.

Makes about 35 large cookies

Butter, softened	1 cup	250 ml
Granulated sugar	1 cup	250 ml
Light brown sugar, packed	1/4 cup	50 ml
Honey	2 Tbsp	30 ml
Large eggs	2	2
Fresh lemon juice	2 Tbsp	30 ml
White rice flour	1 cup	250 ml
sorghum flour	1 cup	250 ml
Coconut flour	1/4 cup	50 ml
Tapioca starch	2 Tbsp	30 ml
Xanthan gum	1 tsp	5 ml
Salt	1 tsp	5 ml
Baking soda	1 tsp	5 ml
Baking powder	½ tsp	2 ml
Lemons, zest of	2	2
Granulated sugar, for dipping		

In stand mixer, cream butter and sugars until fluffy. Add honey, eggs, and lemon juice, beat until everything is fully incorporated and smooth.

In a large bowl, mix together remaining ingredients. Slowly add this dry mix to the mixer bowl, and carefully mix until well incorporated and smooth. Wrap dough in plastic film, chill for 1 hour.

Preheat the oven to 375 F (190 C), line baking sheets with parchment paper.

Roll 1" balls out of the cookie dough. Gently dip the top of each ball into the sugar, arrange dough balls on baking sheets. Leave at least 2" between cookies - they flatten out a fair amount. Gently press the tops of each slightly - flatten JUST enough to prevent the dough from rolling.

Bake for 11-13 minutes. Cookies will look puffy, but flatten out as they cool. Do not over bake! Allow cookies to cool for 2 minutes before removing from baking sheets. Cool completely before storing in an airtight container

Spiced Oatmeal Raisin Cookies

Spiced Oatmeal Raisin Cookies

These are amazing - even better than the original, gluten version. The flour mixture complements and supports the heft of the oats, and it has a wonderful chew to it. Highly addictive comfort food, with a great texture.

Note: While oats are inherently gluten-free, they have a high risk of cross contamination. For this reason, it's best to use oats and oat flour that are certified gluten-free.

Makes about 30 large cookies

Butter, softened	1 cup	250 ml
Light brown sugar, packed	1 cup	250 ml
Granulated sugar	½ cup	125 ml
Large eggs	2	2
Vanilla extract	1 tsp	5 ml
Sorghum flour	½ cup	125 ml
Gluten-free oat flour	½ cup	125 ml
Coconut flour	1/4 cup	50 ml
Tapioca starch	1 Tbsp	15 ml
Xanthan gum	1 tsp	5 ml
Baking soda	1 tsp	5 ml
Ground cinnamon	1 tsp	5 ml
Ground cloves	½ tsp	2 ml
Salt	½ tsp	2 ml
Gluten-free rolled oats	3 cups	750 ml
Raisins	1 ½ cups	375 ml

In stand mixer, cream butter and sugars until fluffy. Add eggs and vanilla extract, beat until everything is fully incorporated and smooth.

In a large bowl, mix together flours, starch, xanthan gum, baking soda, spices, and salt. Slowly add this dry mix to the mixer bowl, and carefully mix until well incorporated and smooth. Add oats and raisins, continue mixing just until well incorporated. Wrap dough in plastic film, chill for 1 hour.

Preheat oven to 350 F (180 C), line baking sheets with parchment paper.

Roll 1" balls out of the cookie dough. Gently dip the top of each ball into the sugar, arrange dough balls on baking sheets. Leave at least 2" between cookies - they flatten out a fair amount. Gently press the tops of each slightly - flatten JUST enough to prevent the dough from rolling.

Bake for 11-13 minutes. Cookies will look puffy, but flatten out as they cool. Do not over bake! Allow cookies to cool for 2 minutes before removing from baking sheets. Cool completely before storing in an airtight container

Peanut Butter Cookies

Peanut Butter Cookies

Peanut butter cookies are one of our favourites, and these don't disappoint . The texture is just.. right. A dense but soft (the way we bake them), satisfying cookie.

If you like your cookies soft, bake for a little less time (I know one friend who goes only one step beyond "raw"!). If you like them a little drier and crispier, bake for an extra minute or two.

Makes about 24 large cookies

Brown rice flour	½ cup	125 ml
Sorghum flour	½ cup	125 ml
Coconut flour	1/4 cup	50 ml
Tapioca starch	2 Tbsp	30 ml
Xanthan gum	1 tsp	5 ml
Baking powder	1 tsp	5 ml
Baking soda	1/4 tsp	1 ml
Salt	1/4 tsp	1 ml
Softened butter	½ cup	125 ml
Peanut butter	½ cup	125 ml
Granulated sugar	½ cup	125 ml
Light brown sugar, packed	½ cup	125 ml
Large eggs	2	2
Vanilla extract	1 tsp	5 ml

Whisk together all dry ingredients (except sugars) until well combined, set aside.

In a stand mixer, cream together butter, peanut butter, sugar, and brown sugar until smooth and fluffy. Add in eggs and vanilla extract, and mix until well incorporated and smooth.

Slowly add dry mix to the mixer bowl, and carefully mix until well incorporated and smooth. Wrap dough in plastic film, chill for 1 hour.

Preheat the oven to 375 F (190 C), line baking sheets with parchment paper.

Roll 1.25" balls out of the cookie dough. Arrange dough balls on baking sheets leaving at least 2" between cookies - they flatten out a fair amount. Gently press the tops of each slightly with a fork.

Bake for 12-14 minutes. Cookies will look puffy, but flatten out as they cool. Do not overbake!

Allow cookies to cool for 2 minutes before removing from baking sheets. Cool completely before storing in an airtight container.

Snickerdoodle Cookies

Snickerdoodle Cookies

Traditional chewy sugar cookie base, with a bit of a sweet bite from the cinnamon. Like any of my chewy cookie recipes, this gets a great texture from the inclusion of a little coconut flour.

If you like yours crispy, cook for an extra minute or two.

Makes about 36 large cookies

Brown rice flour	1 cup	250 ml
Sorghum flour	1 cup	250 ml
Coconut flour	1/4 cup	50 ml
Tapioca starch	2 Tbsp	30 ml
Cream of tartar	1 ½ tsp	7 ml
Xanthan gum	1 tsp	5 ml
Baking soda	1 tsp	5 ml
Salt	½ tsp	2 ml
Butter, softened	1 cup	250 ml
Granulated sugar	1½ cups	375 ml
Large eggs	2	2 ml
Vanilla extract	1 tsp	5 ml
Sugar	1/4 cup	50 ml
Cinnamon	1 Tbsp	15 ml

Whisk together flours, starch, cream of tartar, xanthan gum, baking soda and salt until well combined, set aside.

In a stand mixer, cream together butter and sugar until smooth and fluffy. Add in eggs and vanilla extract, mix until well incorporated and smooth.

Slowly add dry mix to the mixer bowl, and carefully mix until well incorporated and smooth. Wrap dough in plastic film, chill for 1 hour.

Preheat the oven to 375 F (190 C), line baking sheets with parchment paper. In a small bowl, combine remaining sugar with the cinnamon, set aside

Roll 1.25" balls out of the cookie dough, then roll in cinnamon sugar mix. Arrange dough balls on baking sheets leaving at least 2.5" between cookies - they flatten out a fair amount. Gently press the tops of each - flatten JUST enough to prevent the dough from rolling.

Bake for 9-11 minutes. Cookies will look puffy, but flatten out as they cool. Do not overbake!

Allow cookies to cool for 2 minutes before removing from baking sheets. Cool completely before storing in an airtight container.

Meringue Cookies

Meringue Cookies

Meringue cookies are cheap and easy to make, using only a few - really common! - ingredients. They're fun to pipe out, and look so pretty on a holiday sweets platter. They melt in your mouth, with a satisfying texture; as my husband says, it's like popping bubble wrap in your mouth - the bubbly texture as it crumbles and melts.

Use your favourite flavour extract for these, just don't use a flavour OIL - oil will make them deflate.

Makes about 40 large cookies

Large egg whites	6	6
Salt	½ tsp	2 ml
Cream of tartar	½ tsp	2 ml
Granulated sugar	1 ½ cups	375 ml
Extract of choice (NOT oil)	2-3 tsp	10-15 ml
Food colouring, optional		

Preheat oven to 200 F (95 C). Prepare baking sheets by lining with parchment paper. (Do NOT use pan spray, or the same reason you're not using a flavour oil!)

In the bowl of a stand mixer, combine egg whites, salt, and cream of tartar. Using the whisk attachment, whip on high until glossy peaks form. Slowly add in the sugar – a little at a time – and continue whipping until stiff peaks form. Turn off mixer, remove bowl. Gently stir in extract, to taste.

If colouring your meringue, divide mix into as many bowls as you'll be tinting. Add food colouring, stir until desired shade is reached. Spoon each colour into its own pastry bag, tying the large end closed with twine or an elastic band. Clip the pointed end off, and pipe 2-2.5" swirled mounds onto prepared baking sheets, leaving 2" between each.

Alternately, you can do multicoloured meringues: Fit one large pastry bag with a large coupler set and tip of your choice – I used a 4B, large star tip. Carefully feed 2 or 3 of the individual colour bags into this large bag, so that all of the open tips insert almost all the way into the coupler .Be gentle, you don't want to squeeze meringue out of one or both of those bags yet! Use this composite bag to pipe 2-2.5" mounds on the baking sheets, as above.

Bake for 1 hr 30 minutes to 1 hr 45 minutes, or until just starting to get lightly browned. (Note: if it is humid when you make these, it can take more time!). You'll know they are done when they easily lift from the parchment, instead of sticking to it.

Once the time is up, crack the oven door and allow them to cool in the oven for several hours. Store in an airtight container.

Oatmeal Peanut Butter Sandwich Cookies

Oatmeal Peanut Butter Sandwich Cookies

These cookies began as a craving for an off-the-shelf cookie from back home - Pirate Cookies. My husband had never tried them, so I made a gluten-free version... and I was promptly informed that they were very much like a Girl Scout cookie he liked. (After some Googling, it appears he means Do-Si-Dos).

Either way, they turned out amazing, and now disappear FAST whenever I make them. I aimed for a little softer and smoother of a cookie than the source material, because I'm not a fan of dry cookies. If you prefer a crispy cookie, allow to bake for an extra minute or two.

Makes about 30 2" cookies

Gluten-free oat flour	3/4 cup	175 ml
Sorghum flour	1/4 cup	50 ml
Coconut flour	1/4 cup	50 ml
Xanthan gum	1 tsp	5 ml
Baking powder	½ tsp	2 ml
Salt	½ tsp	2 ml
Butter, softened	1/3 cup	75 ml
Granulated sugar	2/3 cup	150 ml
Large egg	1	1
Vanilla extract	1 tsp	5 ml
Corn starch, for rolling.		

Filling: Peanut butter variation of basic filling, page 138

Whisk together dry ingredients (except sugar) until well combined, set aside.

In a stand mixer, cream together butter and sugar until smooth and fluffy. Add in egg, beat well. Add vanilla extract, and mix until well incorporated and smooth. Slowly add dry mix to the mixer bowl, and carefully mix until well incorporated and smooth. Wrap dough in plastic film, chill for 1 hour.

Preheat oven to 350 F (180 C), line baking sheets with parchment paper

Generously sprinkle clean work surface with corn starch, roll dough to 1/8" thick. Use cookie cutters to cut out rounds, place cookies 1" apart on greased baking sheets. Bake cookies for 8-10 minutes, or until bottoms look lightly golden.

Allow cookies to cool on baking sheets for at least 5 minutes before moving. Cookies need to cool completely before filling.

To fill: Spoon prepared filling into a pastry bag. Cut the tip off and pipe about a small amount of filling onto the bottom of one cookie. Flip over, top with another cookie.

Basic Sandwich Cookies

Basic Sandwich Cookies

These sandwich cookies taste far better than store bought "regular" sandwich cookies, and can be customized many different ways. Missing those maple sandwich cookies? Swap maple extract for the vanilla in both cookie and filling. Lemon? Go for it - just use lemon extract. Chocolate? Swap out 1/4 cup of the brown rice flour for cocoa powder.

Makes about 25-30 2" cookies

Brown rice flour	½ cup	125 ml
Sorghum flour	½ cup	125 ml
Coconut flour	2 Tbsp	30 ml
Tapioca starch	1 Tbsp	15 ml
Xanthan gum	1 tsp	5 ml
Baking powder	½ tsp	2 ml
Salt	½ tsp	2 ml
Butter, softened	1/3 cup	75 ml
Granulated sugar	2/3 cup	150 ml
Large egg	1	1
Vanilla extract	1 tsp	5 ml
Corn starch, for rolling.		

Whisk together all dry ingredients (except sugar) until well combined, set aside.

In a stand mixer, cream together butter and sugar until smooth and fluffy. Add in egg, beat well. Add vanilla extract, and mix until well incorporated and smooth.

Slowly add dry mix to the mixer bowl, and carefully mix until well incorporated and smooth. Wrap dough in plastic film, chill for 1 hour.

Preheat oven to 350 F (180 C), line baking sheets with parchment paper

Generously sprinkle clean work surface with corn starch, roll dough to 1/8" thick. Use cookie cutters to cut out rounds, place cookies 1" apart on greased baking sheets.

Bake cookies for 8-10 minutes, or until bottoms look lightly golden. Allow cookies to cool on baking sheets for at least 5 minutes before moving. Cookies need to cool completely before filling.

To fill: Spoon prepared filling (next page) into a pastry bag. Cut the tip off and pipe about a small amount of filling onto the bottom of one cookie. Flip over, top with another cookie.

Basic Filling

Butter, softened	1/4 cup	50 ml
Vanilla extract	½ tsp	2 ml
Salt	pinch	pinch
Icing (Powdered) sugar	2 cups	500 ml
Water	2 Tbsp	30 ml

Whip butter until smooth. Add vanilla extract and salt, and mix until incorporated.

Slowly add powdered sugar a bit at a time, until incorporated completely. Beat on high for 1 minute – mixture will be very, very thick.

Lower mixer speed to lowest setting, and slowly add water. Once incorporated, check for consistency. Add more water or powdered sugar to achieve the consistency you want.

Variation: Use Nutella or peanut butter instead of butter!

Chocolate Filling

Butter, softened	1/4 cup	50 ml
Vanilla extract	½ tsp	2 ml
Salt	pinch	pinch
Icing (Powdered) sugar	1 3/4 cups	425 ml
Cocoa powder	1/4 cup	50 ml
Water	2 Tbsp	30 ml

Whip butter until smooth. Add vanilla extract and salt, and mix until incorporated.

Whisk together powdered sugar and cocoa. Slowly add powdered sugar mixture to butter a bit at a time, until incorporated completely. Beat on high for 1 minute – mixture will be very, very thick.

Lower mixer speed to lowest setting, and slowly add water. Once incorporated, check for consistency. Add more water or powdered sugar to achieve the consistency you want.

Variation: Use Nutella or peanut butter instead of butter!

Graham Crackers

A few months before starting work on this book, my husband and I went "camping" .. by which I mean we rented a tiny little 1 room cabin and cooked our food over a fire pit outside. It was great... aside from the S'mores we made. I'd never actually done S'mores before, so my husband showed me how it was done... but with gluten-free graham crackers.

Oh... those crackers were terrible. I actually picked them off the marshmallow and tossed them, finding them completely inedible. To add insult to injury, we'd ordered them online, as we couldn't find any gluten-free ones locally - they weren't cheap!

So, obviously I needed to come up with a recipe for them. The problem with graham crackers, specifically, is that they use a special type of flour - graham flour - that really doesn't have a gluten-free replacement. Just using an all-purpose mix (as store bought ones do) of the regular gluten-free flours won't give you anything resembling that unique flavour from the graham flour.

Enter rice bran! I'm not big on having weird ingredients in this book, but for something like this, I'll make an exception. Rice bran and a little flax meal, combined with the flours I've chosen for this, create a mix that is pretty much indistinguishable from the taste and texture of graham flour product. Add in carefully planned quantities of honey, molasses, and cinnamon, and BOOM - proper "graham" crackers!

Just try to use good chocolate if you make S'mores off these. The traditional stuff is gross, in my spoiled Canadian opinion. (Chocolate should not be gritty!)

Makes about 50 2.5" square crackers

Rice Bran	1 cup	250 ml
Sorghum flour	½ cup	125 ml
Light buckwheat flour	½ cup	125 ml
Corn starch	½ cup	125 ml
Light brown sugar, packed	½ cup	125 ml
Baking powder	1 Tbsp	15 ml
Flax meal	1 Tbsp	15 ml
Xanthan gum	1 tsp	5 ml
Salt	3/4 tsp	3ml
Baking soda	½ tsp	2 ml
Cinnamon	1/8-1/4 tsp	½-1 ml
Molasses	1 Tbsp	15 ml
Honey	2 Tbsp	30 ml
Vanilla extract	½ tsp	2 ml
Cold butter	½ cup	125 ml
Cold Milk	1/3 cup	75 ml
Corn starch, for rolling		

Granulated sugar	1 Tbsp	15 ml
Cinnamon	1/4 tsp	1 ml

Measure bran, flours, corn starch, brown sugar, baking powder, flax meal, xanthan gum, salt, baking soda, and spices into the bowl of your food processor, blitz to combine. Add molasses, honey, and vanilla extract, blitz once more to combine.

Add butter, blitz a few times until mixture resembles gravel. Stream in milk as you run the food processor, just long enough to start to bring it together as a dough – you may need to use a little more or less milk. Do NOT over-process it!

Remove dough from processor, knead lightly to bring it together as a ball. Wrap in plastic film, chill for 1 hour.

Preheat oven to 350 F (180 C), line baking sheets with parchment paper

Generously sprinkle clean work surface with corn starch, roll dough to 1/8" thick. Use cookie cutters or a pizza wheel to cut out squares or rectangles, place graham crackers 1" apart on greased baking sheets. Prick top of each cookie several times with a fork.

Mix together sugar and cinnamon, sprinkle over prepared cookies.

Bake for about 12 minutes. Allow cookies to cool for 5 minutes before removing from baking sheets. Cool completely before storing in an airtight container

Graham Crackers

Polvorones

Polvorones

Polvorones - a nut based Mexican cookie - were a popular request, when I asked readers "what would you like a recipe for?".

When I first made this recipe up, I'd never had Russian tea cakes before. As soon as I had my husband try the uncooked batter, he declared that they were BANG ON for Russian Tea Cakes, grabbed the bowl, and left the room! In Googling, I found that they were the same basic idea. The Russian version tends to use hazelnuts, while Mexican version walnuts or pecans. Also, the Mexican version tends to have a little cinnamon in the powdered sugar coating.

Either way, these have a great "melt in your mouth", slightly crumbly texture, with a nice, nutty flavour.

Walnuts, pecans, or almonds	1 cup	250 ml
Sorghum flour	½ cup	125 ml
Light buckwheat flour	½ cup	125 ml
Corn starch	½ cup	125 ml
Coconut flour	1/4 cup	40 ml
Icing (Powdered) sugar	1 cup	250 ml
Salt	pinch	pinch
Cold butter	½ cup	125 ml
Shortening	½ cup	125 ml
Large egg	1	1
Additional powdered sugar for dusting		
Cinnamon, optional		

Place nuts into food processor, blitz until finely ground. Measure flours, starch, powdered sugar, and salt into the bowl of your food processor, blitz to combine. Add butter, shortening, and egg, blitz a few times until mixture resembles fine gravel.

Remove dough from processor, knead lightly to bring it together as a ball. Wrap in plastic film, chill for 30 minutes.

Preheat oven to 325 F (165 C), line two baking sheets with parchment paper.

Quickly and carefully roll cookie dough into walnut sized balls - don't over handle the dough!

Arrange cookie balls onto prepared baking sheets, leaving at least an inch between each cookie. Bake for 18-20 minutes, or until just starting to turn golden. As cookies are baking, place a cup or two of powdered sugar into a large mixing bowl. If you'd like to use cinnamon, add 1-3 tsp of it to your powdered sugar, to taste. Once cookies are baked, remove from oven and allow to cool for 5 minutes or so.

Working with a few cookies at a time, gently toss warm cookies in powdered sugar before placing on a cooling rack. Allow cookies to cool completely, before dusting with more powdered sugar and storing in an airtight container.

Pizzelles

Pizzelles

Traditionally, Pizzelles make use of anise extract - a black licorice flavour. While I love it, it's not for everybody - so feel free to substitute vanilla or lemon extract, to suit your own tastes!

We love the texture that the pizzelle press imparts to the cookie. Almost like a waffle cone - and could totally be used as one, if you wrap it around a cone form instead of a dowel form. (If you're making cannoli or waffle cones with it, definitely use vanilla to flavour them!)

Makes 28-30 4" pizzelles

Large eggs	3	3
Granulated sugar	3/4 cup	175 ml
Extract - Anise or vanilla	1 tsp	5 ml
Salt	½ tsp	2 ml
Milk	1 Tbsp	15 ml
Sorghum flour	1 cup	250 ml
White rice flour	1/4 cup	50 ml
Corn starch	1/3 cup	75 ml
Coconut flour	2 Tbsp	30 ml
Baking powder	2 tsp	10 ml
Xanthan gum	½ tsp	2 ml
Unsalted butter, melted	½ cup	125 ml
Icing (Powdered) sugar, optional		

In a medium mixing bowl, beat together eggs, sugar, extract, and salt until thick and pale yellow. Add milk, whisk until well combined. In a separate bowl, whisk together flours, starch, baking powder, and xanthan gum until well combined.

Add the flour mix to the wet ingredients, whisking until smooth. Allow to sit for 10 minutes, start preheating your pizzelle press.

Once the time is up, add melted butter, whisk once again until well combined.

Spray pizzelle press with nonstick spray if the manufacturer's directions call for it. Follow the manufacturer directions to cook your pizzelle - it will generally need about 1 Tbsp of batter per pizzelle, cooked for between 45 seconds and 2 minutes.

If you want normal pizzelles, transfer to a wire rack to cool. Allow to cool fully before dusting with powdered sugar, if desired.

If you want to cut them into wedges, use clean kitchen scissors to do so while they're still hot from the press. Cool and dust with powdered sugar, if desired.

If you want to make cannoli or cones, wrap the hot pizzelles around an appropriate mold - metal cones or dowels. We bought ours on Amazon. Allow pizzelles to cool fully before removing from cone/dowel.

Cannoli

Traditionally, cannoli dough is rolled very thin, wrapped around a metal dowel and deep fried. Pizzelles formed onto tubes are not only a little healthier of an alternative, they're easier to make, and just work better than deep frying gluten-free dough.

10 prepared cannoli shells, page 145
Chocolate of choice
Chopped pistachios, sprinkles, etc

Melt chocolate. Dip edges of each cannoli into melted chocolate, allowing excess to drip off before dipping immediately into chopped nuts, sprinkles, etc.

Arrange dipped cannoli shells onto a parchment lined baking sheet, chill until set.

Cannoli Filling

Makes enough to fill 8-10 cannoli

Ricotta cheese, drained well	1 cup	250 ml
Mascarpone cheese	8 oz	250 g
Heavy whipping cream	1/4 cup	50 ml
Icing (powdered) sugar	2/3 cup	150 ml
Vanilla extract	1 tsp	5 ml
Lemon, zest of	1	1

In a stand mixer, combine drained ricotta, Mascarpone, and heavy whipping cream. Beat on low until well combined, then whip at a higher speed for 2 minutes.

Turn speed down to low, add powdered sugar, vanilla and lemon zest, beat just until combined.

Carefully spoon mixture into a pastry bag. Cut the tip of the bag off, insert into one side of a chilled cannoli shell, and pipe full of filling. Remove bag, pipe additional into the opposite side of the shell.

Repeat for remaining cannoli shells, until all filling is used up.

Cannoli

147

Unicorn Poop Cookies

A few years ago, I was presented with an interesting challenge. We were headed to a party for some of our more.. uh, COLOURFUL … friends, and it was decided that "unicorn poop" cookies would be perfect for the occasion. We'd all seen these floating around pinterest, and found them to be good for a laugh.

As I was the one to bake them, I would do them gluten-free. Problem? One of those friends is severely allergic to coconut, and coconut flour is my big secret ingredient to making gluten-free cookies with great taste and texture. CRAP!

So, I developed this recipe to work around both of our allergies, while still providing a great tasting cookie with a nice soft/chewy texture. I flavoured them with blood orange extract, after discovering that I didn't have any lemon extract. They smelled completely insane throughout the whole process, and were a big hit at the party!

Makes 24 LARGE poops. I mean cookies.

Brown rice flour	1 cup	250 ml
Sorghum flour	½ cup	125 ml
Light/white buckwheat flour	3/4 cup	175 ml
Tapioca starch	1/4 cup	50 ml
Xanthan gum	2 tsp	10 ml
Baking powder	1 tsp	5 ml
Salt	½ tsp	2 ml
Cream cheese, softened	4 oz	125 g
Butter, softened	½ cup	125 ml
Granulated sugar	1 ½ cup	375 ml
Large eggs	2	2
Extract of choice	1 tsp	5 ml
Gel food colouring – I use Americolor *		
Sparkle gel, edible glitter, etc *		

Whisk together all dry ingredients (except sugar) until well combined, set aside.

In a stand mixer, beat together cream cheese, butter and sugar until smooth and fluffy. Add in eggs and extract, mix until well incorporated and smooth. Slowly add dry mix to the mixer bowl, and carefully mix until well incorporated and smooth.

Divide dough evenly into as many pieces as you want colours – I think 5-6 works best. Colour each with food colouring until desired colour is reached, and dough is uniformly coloured. I wanted vibrant, but pastel would be pretty with this, too. Just make sure the colours look good with each other!

Wrap each colour of dough separately in plastic film, chill for one hour.

Preheat oven to 350 F (180 C), line 2 large baking sheets with parchment paper.

Divide each ball of cookie dough into 4 roughly equal sized lumps. Roll each new ball into a long log shape.

Taking 1 log of each colour, position a set of logs together, then roll into one large rainbow log. Repeat 3 more times, to make 4 large logs.

Cut each large log in half, and then each half into 3 equal pieces. You will now have 24 small logs:

Roll each small log into a longer long, and twist into a turd shape. Have as much fun with this as you can with sculpting poops!

Arrange cookie turds evenly across the two baking sheets. Bake cookies 1 sheet at a time for 15-17 minutes, or until bottoms look lightly golden. Allow cookies to cool on cookie sheets for at least 5 minutes before moving. Allow cookies to cool completely before decorating with sparkle gel, edible glitter, etc.

* As with all gluten-free baking, be sure that any individual ingredients you use are also gluten-free. Americolor is gluten-free, as is the brand of edible glitter we used.

Unicorn Poop Cookies

Sopaipillas Pasadas

Sopaipillas Pasadas

When I was first toying with the idea of developing a second "Beyond Flour" book, my friend Samantha suggested the inclusion of sopaipillas pasadas.

Samantha travels a LOT with her Eurovision blogging - ESC Insight - but as "worldly" as my own culinary experience has been (growing up in Canada!)... I'd never heard of them. Her description sounded amazing though, so here we are.

These are a deep fried pastry from Chile - a street food that is especially popular on cold, rainy days. The pastry itself it flavoured with pumpkin, and it's served with a thick, dark sauce that's flavoured with orange peel and cloves. YUM!

I had to do a ton of research on these, not being able to replicate from my own experience. Descriptions and photos of the sauce and pastry, traditional methods of making it, etc. I had to figure out the closest equivalent to chancaca - lumps of unrefined sugar - that would be easily accessible in North American grocery stores.

In the end, I've developed something got the seal of approval from Samantha - it's always great to watch someone's face as they indulge in a treat they haven't been able to get in years!

Dough:

Masa flour	3/4 cup	175 ml
Buckwheat flour	3/4 cup	175 ml
Potato starch	½ cup	125 ml
White rice flour	1/4 cup	50 ml
Sweet rice flour	1/4 cup	50 ml
Baking powder	2 ½ tsp	12 ml
Salt	1 tsp	5 ml
Cold butter	1/4 cup	50 ml
Large egg	1	1
Pumpkin puree (Not pie filling!)	1 cup	250 ml
Water	1/4 cup	50 ml
Corn starch for rolling		
Oil for frying		

Sauce:

Large orange	1	1
Light brown sugar, packed	2 cups	500 ml
Water	1 cup	250 ml
Cinnamon	½ tsp	2 ml
Whole cloves	3	3

Measure flours, starch, baking powder, and salt into the bowl of your food processor, blitz to combine.

Add butter and egg, blitz a few times until mixture resembles gravel. Add pumpkin, pulse just to combine.

Stream in JUST enough cold water - as you run the food processor - to bring it together as a dough – you may need to use a little more or less water. Do NOT over-process it! It will be a little sticky, that's fine.

Remove dough from processor, knead lightly to bring it together as a ball. Wrap in plastic film, rest on counter for 30 minutes. While dough is resting, make your sauce:

Use a vegetable peeler to peel the orange - you want just the outer, orange peel, with no white pith.

Place orange peel - along with remaining sauce ingredients- into a medium saucepan, bring just to a boil. Reduce heat to medium, simmer for 20 minutes or so, until sauce is nice and thick. Strain off orange peel and cloves.

To assemble:

Start heating your oil to 350 F (180 C) – you'll want about 2" of oil in your pot or deep fryer.

Scatter some corn starch over your - clean! - work surface. Roll dough out to about 1/4" thick. Use a glass to cut rounds of dough that are about 2.5" in diameter. Use a fork to prick holes in the top surface of each round.

Fry a few at a time for a minute or two per side, until nicely golden - not brown.

Use a slotted spoon to transfer fried sopaipillas to platter lined with paper towels.   Place drained sopaipillas in the sauce for a minute before serving, or arrange on a plate and drizzle generously with sauce.

Serve immediately.

Earl Grey Pie

This is an elegant pie that isn't cloyingly sweet - the Earl Grey flavour comes through well, and is really well suited for use in a pie!

We served it for some friends, and one of them - Derek - was almost in tears as he declared that "Everything is perfect with the world" after the first bite. When another friend joined us later, He told her that when she tries the pie, "The gates of heaven will open, and you will see everything".

So. That happened.

Crust:

Light buckwheat flour	½ cup	125 ml
Sorghum flour	1/4 cup	50 ml
Sweet rice flour	1/4 cup	50 ml
Corn starch	1/4 cup	50 ml
Granulated sugar	1 Tbsp	15 ml
Xanthan gum	1 tsp	5 ml
Cream cheese	4 oz	125 g
Cold butter	1/4 cup	50 m
Lemon, zest of	1	1
Large egg	1	1
Cold water	1/4 cup	50 ml

Filling:

Large eggs	2	2
Granulated sugar	½ cup	125 ml
Corn starch	1/3 cup	75 ml
Salt	1/4 tsp	1 ml
Milk	1 cup	250 ml
Heavy cream	1 cup	250 ml
Earl Grey tea bags	3	3
Butter	2 Tbsp	30 ml

Whipped cream, for serving

Measure flours, corn starch, sugar, and xanthan gum into the bowl of your food processor, blitz to combine. Add cream cheese, butter, lemon zest and egg, blitz a few times until mixture resembles gravel.

Stream in cold water as you run the food processor, just long enough to start to bring it together as a dough – you may need to use a little more or less water. Do NOT over-process it!

Remove dough from processor, knead lightly to bring it together as a ball. Wrap in plastic film, chill for 1 hour.

Preheat oven to 450 F (230 C), lightly dust your work surface with extra corn starch.

Roll your crust out to about 1/4" thick. Line a pie pan with the crust, trim the edges of the crust to only slightly longer than the edge of the pie plate. Use your fingers to crimp/ruffle the edge of the pie.

Use a fork to prick some holes on the bottom of the crust. Chill in fridge for 15 minutes.

Once chilled, bake pie crust for 10-12 minutes, or until golden brown. Remove from oven, allow to cool to room temperature while you prepare the filling.

Whisk eggs together with sugar until fluffy and pale yellow. Add cornstarch and salt, whisk until incorporated and smooth. Set aside.

In a small saucepan, bring milk and cream just to the start of a boil. Remove from heat, add tea bags, steep for 5 minutes. Remove tea bags, squeezing out excess liquid back into the pot. Bring cream up JUST to a boil once again.

Measure about 1/4 cup of the hot cream mixture, and stream slowly into egg mixture while whisking. Continue streaming liquid and whisking until it is completely incorporated, and mixture is smooth. Repeat with another 1/4 cup of hot cream.

Remove saucepan from heat, pour remaining egg mixture into cream mixture, whisking constantly. Once fully incorporated and smooth, return to heat. Turn heat to medium-low. Continue whisking mixture constantly, cooking until mixture is very thick. Remove from heat, stir in butter until melted and smooth. Cool to room temperature.

Spoon filling into prepared crust, cover with plastic wrap. Chill until set, about 3 hours.

To serve, top with whipped cream.

Earl Grey Pie

Pumpkin Pie with Maple Cream

Pumpkin Pie with Maple Cream

Shortly after Beyond Flour came out, I was to make a pumpkin pie for a Thanksgiving get together. I put this one together, and it quickly became a favourite! The crust is slightly sweeter than my normal crust, and spiced up a little to accent the filling.

I use a bit of cream cheese in the filling, because I love the texture it imparts. No worries - this is definitely a pumpkin pie, rather than anything even bordering on cheesecake. It contains a generous dose of maple syrup, because I AM a walking cliche at times. (Eh? I feel like I need to punctuate that with an "eh"!)

This tastes as good as it looks, with or without the maple cream topping (which I adore!). The crust makes enough for 2 normal sized crusts, while the filling makes enough for 1 deep dish pie, 2 slightly smaller pies, or a normal pie and a few tarts. I usually do a normal sized pie and a few tarts, using up both the entire recipe of dough, and the entire batch of filling.

White rice flour	3/4 cup	175 ml
Light buckwheat flour	3/4 cup	175 ml
Millet flour	½ cup	125 ml
Sweet rice flour	1/4 cup	50 ml
Corn starch	1/4 cup	50 ml
Light brown sugar, packed	1/4 cup	50 ml
Xanthan gum	2 tsp	10 ml
Cinnamon	1/4 tsp	1 ml
Ground nutmeg	pinch	pinch
Ground cloves	pinch	pinch
Cream cheese	8 oz	250 g
Cold butter	½ cup	125 ml
Large egg	1	1
Cold water	1/3 cup+	75 ml+
Cream cheese, softened	8 oz	250 g
Light brown sugar, packed	½ cup	125 ml
Large eggs	4	4
Pumpkin puree (fresh or canned)	2 cups	500 ml
Heavy cream	½ cup	125 ml
Maple syrup	½ cup	125 ml
Vanilla extract	2 tsp	10 ml
Cinnamon	1 tsp	5 ml
Ground ginger	1 tsp	5 ml
Ground cloves	1/4 tsp	1 ml
Salt	1/4 tsp	1 ml

Measure flours, corn starch, brown sugar, xanthan gum, and spices into the bowl of your food processor, blitz to combine. Add cream cheese, butter, and egg, blitz a few times until mixture resembles gravel.

Stream in cold water as you run the food processor, just long enough to start to bring it together as a dough – you may need to use a little more or less water. Do NOT over-process it!

Remove dough from processor, knead lightly to bring it together as a ball. Wrap in plastic film, chill for 1 hour.

Divide dough in half*, Roll your crust (s) out to about 1/4" thick. Line a pie pan with one crust, trim the edges of the crust to only slightly longer than the edge of the pie plate. Use your fingers to crimp/ruffle the edge of the pie.

Use a fork to prick some holes on the bottom of the crust. Chill in fridge until ready to bake.

* If you are only using half of the dough, tightly wrap the second half of the dough and freeze it until the day before you want to use it. Allow it to thaw on your counter, then proceed as described above.

Preheat oven to 350 F (180 C).

In a stand mixer (or in a bowl with an electric mixer), cream together cream cheese and brown sugar. Once smooth, add remaining ingredients and mix just until smooth. Do not over-beat it!

Take crust out of the fridge. Gently cover edge of crust with aluminum foil, bake for 15 minutes. Remove from oven, discard foil, fill with pumpkin mixture. Transfer to oven, bake for 45-50 minutes or so, until center is set. Remove from heat and allow to cool fully before serving.

Serve as is, with whipped cream, or with maple cream:

Maple Cream

Very cold heavy whipping cream	1 cup	250 ml
Maple syrup	2 Tbsp	30 ml
Salt	pinch	pinch

Using a stand mixer with a whisk attachment or an electric hand mixer, whip cream until soft peaks form.

Add maple syrup and salt, continue whipping until it reaches desired consistency. Serve immediately.

Mini Cinnamon Buns

These are kind of a cross between a bun and a soft cookie, using a pie dough type crust. The tender, flaky dough that gives you the taste of cinnamon buns, without all the effort of yeast bread. I designed them this way to avoid needing the structure that full sized buns require - cinnamon bun taste, without the time commitment!

Makes 24 Mini buns

White rice flour	3/4 cup	175 ml
Buckwheat flour	3/4 cup	175 ml
Millet flour	½ cup	125 ml
Coconut flour	1/4 cup	50 ml
Corn starch	1/4 cup	50 ml
Granulated sugar	2 Tbsp	30 ml
Baking powder	2 tsp	10 ml
Xanthan gum	1 tsp	5 ml
Salt	½ tsp	2 ml
Cream cheese	8 oz	250 g
Cold butter	½ cup	125 ml
Large egg	1	1
Cold water	2/3 cup	150 ml
Granulated sugar	3/4 cup	175 ml
Cinnamon	2 Tbsp	30 ml
Melted butter	½ cup	125 ml

Glaze:

Butter, softened	2 Tbsp	30 ml
Vanilla extract	1 tsp	5 ml
Hot water	3 Tbsp	45 ml
Icing (powdered) sugar	~2 cups	~ 500 ml

Measure flours, corn starch, sugar, baking powder, xanthan gum, and salt into the bowl of your food processor, blitz to combine. Add cream cheese, butter, and egg, blitz a few times until mixture resembles gravel. Stream in cold water as you run the food processor, just long enough to start to bring it together as a sticky dough – you may need to use a little more or less water.

Remove dough from processor, knead lightly to bring it together as a ball. Wrap in plastic film, chill for 1 hour.

Preheat oven to 375 F (190 C). In a small bowl, mix together sugar and cinnamon.

Divide dough in half. Lightly dust clean work surface with corn starch, roll one piece of dough out to about 10 x 15". Use a pastry brush to spread melted butter all over the dough, then sprinkle entire surface with about half of the sugar mixture.

Starting with one of the longer edges, tightly roll the dough up. Using a very sharp knife, slice the roll into 12 even rounds. Repeat with the second piece of dough.

Generously grease or spray a mini muffin baking pan. Place 1 roll into each muffin void, brush tops with remaining melted butter.

Bake for 22-25 minutes or until golden brown. Allow mini buns to cool for a few minutes while you make the glaze:

Mix together softened butter, vanilla extract, hot water, and about ½ cup of powdered sugar, whisking until smooth. Add remaining powdered sugar, about 1/4 cup at a time, until you have a thick, smooth paste.

Spread over hot cinnamon buns, allowing it to melt and ooze a little. Best served warm.

Mini Cinnamon Buns

Rustic Cardamom Pear Tart

I asked my husband what he had to say about this recipe for a description, and he just went "OH MY GOD!". It may look "rustic", but this is a really fabulous, easy to make dessert that'll make an impression. The dough holds up very well without being gummy or chewy. It's not an overly sweet dough, but the sprinkling of sugar and cardamom on the edges brings not only a little sweetness and flavour, but a crystalline crunch.

Cardamom and pear are two flavours that work really well together, creating a warmly spiced, rich and complex dish. We love it warm, with a scoop of vanilla bean ice cream on top!

Note: Not a fan of pears? Try this recipe with apples and cinnamon (and a pinch of cloves and nutmeg), or with peaches!

Light buckwheat flour	½ cup	125 ml
Sorghum flour	1/4 cup	50 ml
Sweet rice flour	1/4 cup	50 ml
Corn starch	1/4 cup	50 ml
Granulated sugar	1 Tbsp	15 ml
Xanthan gum	1 tsp	5 ml
Cardamom	pinch	pinch
Cream cheese	4 oz	125 g
Cold butter	1/4 cup	50 m
Large egg	1	1
Cold water	1/4 cup	50 ml
Large pears	3	3
Lemon juice	1 Tbsp	15 ml
Honey	1 Tbsp	15 ml
Cornstarch	2 Tbsp	30 ml
Granulated sugar	2 Tbsp	30 ml
Cardamom	1 tsp	5 ml
Salt	pinch	pinch
Chopped pistachios, optional	1/4 cup	50 ml
Large egg	1	1
Water	1 Tbsp	15 ml
Granulated sugar	2 Tbsp	30 ml
Cardamom	1/4 tsp	1 ml

Measure flours, corn starch, sugar, xanthan gum, and cardamom into the bowl of your food processor, blitz to combine. Add cream cheese, butter, and egg, blitz a few times until mixture resembles gravel. Stream in cold water as you run the food processor, just long enough to start to bring it together as a dough – you may need to use a little more or less water. Do NOT over-process it!

Remove dough from processor, knead lightly to bring it together as a ball. Wrap in plastic film, chill for 1 hour.

Peel pears, core and slice thinly - you want about 4 cups of slices. Place pear slices in a large bowl, toss with lemon juice and honey. Sprinkle pears with cornstarch, sugar, cardamom, and salt, toss gently to combine and coat.

Preheat oven to 425 F (220 C).

Lay a sheet of parchment paper out on a clear working surface, lightly dust with cornstarch. Roll dough out into a rough circle that's about 10" in diameter. Carefully transfer parchment paper and dough round to a baking sheet.

Arrange pears in the middle of the dough round, leaving a 2" border around the edge. Sprinkle with pistachios, if using. Fold dough border up and over onto the pears - remember, this is "rustic", so it doesn't have to be even, or even pretty!

Whisk together egg and water, brush over outer crust of the tart. Mix together sugar and cardamom, sprinkle over the egg washed crust. Bake for 15 minutes. Without opening the oven door, turn heat down to 350 and continue to bake for another 20 minutes.

Slice and serve warm.

Rustic Cardamom Pear Tart

Butter Tart Bars

Butter Tart Bars

These bars are great - a much quicker and easier way to indulge that "I would do some pretty depraved things for a butter tart" urge that many Canadians abroad tend to get!

The crust holds up really well - nice and robust, holding up to the weight of the filling, while also providing a nice contrast to that filling.

Makes an 8 x 8 pan of bars

Sorghum flour	2/3 cup	150 ml
Sweet rice flour	1/3 cup	75 ml
Corn starch	1/4 cup	50 ml
Sugar	1/4 cup	50 ml
Xanthan gum	½ tsp	2 ml
Butter	½ cup	125 ml
Large egg	1	1
Brown sugar, packed	1 cup	250 ml
Corn starch	1 Tbsp	15 ml
Sorghum flour	1 Tbsp	15 ml
Baking powder	½ tsp	2 ml
Salt	1/4 tsp	1 ml
Butter, melted	1/4 cup	50 ml
Eggs, beaten	3	3
Maple syrup	2 Tbsp	30 ml
Vanilla extract	1 tsp	5 ml
Raisins	1 cup	250 ml
Walnuts, optional	½ cup	125 ml

Preheat oven to 350 F (180 C), Line an 8x8" pan with parchment paper

Combine flours, corn starch, sugar, and xanthan gum in a food processor. Add butter and egg, blitz until finely crumbly. Spread mixture out in prepared pan, distributing evenly. Firmly press to create a level crust. Bake for 15 minutes.

In a medium mixing bowl, whisk together brown sugar, corn starch, sorghum flour, baking powder and salt. Add butter, eggs, maple syrup and vanilla, whisk to combine well. Add raisins, stir. Pour mixture over crust.

Bake bars for 20 minutes, remove from heat, cool to room temperature.

Once cool, transfer to fridge and chill for an hour before cutting into squares.

Variation: To double the recipe, use a 9x13" pan. Do the initial crust bake for 20 minutes, and second bake for 25-30 minutes

Carrot Cake

Carrot cake is such an iconic, traditional thing.. And it's also the easiest cake to hide "gluten free" in - as long as you have the flours and moisture proportions right! With all the flavours and textures going on in carrot cake, it's really easy to forget the fact that this one is gluten free!

Just remember: As with most cakes, "Cold cake is dry cake"! Let this come to room temperature before serving!

Shortening		
Light buckwheat flour	1 cup	250 ml
Granulated sugar	3/4 cup	175 ml
Light brown sugar, packed	3/4 cup	175 ml
Sorghum flour	½ cup	125 ml
Coconut flour	1/4 cup	50 ml
Sweet rice flour	1/4 cup	50 ml
Baking powder	2 tsp	10 ml
Cinnamon	2 tsp	10 ml
Baking soda	1 tsp	5 ml
Salt	1 tsp	5 ml
Nutmeg	½ tsp	2 ml
Ground cloves	pinch	pinch
Large eggs	4	4
Vegetable oil	3/4 cup	175 ml
Vanilla extract	1 tsp	5 ml
Freshly grated carrots	2 cups	500 ml
Crushed pineapple (not drained)	1 cup	250 ml
Chopped walnuts	½ cup	125 ml
Golden raisins (optional*)	½ cup	125 ml

Preheat oven to 350°F (180°C). Liberally grease a 9" x 13" pan with shortening, set aside.

Combine flours, sugars, baking powder, spices, baking soda, and salt in a large mixing bowl or stand mixer. Add in eggs, oil, and vanilla extract, beating until smooth. Add carrots, pineapple, chopped walnuts, and raisins, mixing until well incorporated.

Pour batter into prepared cake pan. Bake until golden and knife inserted into center of batter comes out clean and cake springs back – about 40 minutes.

Allow to cool 10-15 minutes before turning cake out onto baking rack to cool. Once cake is cool enough to handle, wrap tightly with plastic wrap.

Allow cake to sit overnight, before frosting with cream cheese frosting, next page.

* If you include raisins, add an extra 1/4 cup canned pineapple.

166

Cream Cheese Frosting

Butter, softened	1/4 cup	50 ml
Cream cheese, softened	8 oz	250 g
Icing (powdered) sugar	1- 2 lbs	500-1000 g
Milk	2 Tbsp	30 ml
Vanilla Extract	2 tsp	10 ml

Whip butter and cream cheese together until smooth and fluffy.

Slowly add powdered sugar a little bit at a time, until fully incorporated. Beat on high for 1 minute - mixture will be very, very thick.

Lower mixer speed to lowest setting, and slowly add the milk. Beat until fully incorporated and smooth. Add vanilla extract, beating until smooth. Check the consistency, add more milk or powdered sugar to achieve the consistency you want or need.

Carrot Cake

Chocolate Dessert Ravioli

Chocolate Dessert Ravioli

This is one of those recipes that actually works BETTER as a gluten-free recipe, than my original version. The use of fats and starches in this create a dough that is super easy to work with, and doesn't have the frustrations I find with making normal chocolate pasta - cocoa tends to dry out the pasta, so it can be fussy to reach a balance. The use of starches holds moisture in, creating a dough that doesn't break as easily.

Who ever expected to say that of gluten-free dough?

This is a fancy dessert that really allows for a great mix of flavours and textures - you have the rich, not-too-sweet pasta dough, the semi sweet, slightly salty filling, and then the creamy sweetness of the sauce, all coming together for a complex, elegant dessert. Pictured, we made a vanilla ricotta filling and Kahlua cream sauce.

Makes about 20 ravioli

Sour cream	½ cup	125 ml
Large eggs	2	2
Warm milk	2 Tbsp	30 ml
Sorghum flour	½ cup	125 ml
Tapioca starch	1/3 cup	75 ml
Sweet rice flour	1/3 cup	75 ml
Cocoa powder	1/3 cup	75 ml
Granulated sugar	1 Tbsp	15 ml
Xanthan gum	1 tsp	5 ml
Salt	1/4 tsp	1 ml

In a food processor or stand mixer, blitz/beat sour cream, eggs, and milk together until well combined.

In a separate bowl, whisk together remaining ingredients until well combined. Add to wet ingredients, blitz/beat until a sticky dough comes together. Wrap dough in plastic film, allow to rest on counter for 45 minutes. While waiting, work on the filling:

Ricotta Cheese Filling

Ricotta cheese, well drained	8 oz	250 g
Granulated sugar	1-2 Tbsp	15-30 ml
Liqueur of choice	1 Tbsp	15 ml
OR		
Extract of choice	1 tsp	5 ml

Combine ingredients, stirring till well incorporated. Chill until use.

To assemble:

Lightly dust work surface with cocoa powder. Roll dough as thin as possible – about 1/16".

Use a round cookie cutter or rim of a glass – 3" or so in diameter– to cut rounds from the dough. Use a pastry brush to brush a little water around the edge of half the rounds.

Mound 1-2 tsp (5-10 ml) of filling into the middle of each of theses rounds, top with one of the remaining rounds. Press down lightly, squeezing excess air out.

Carefully seal each raviolo, pinching the edges together around the entire seam.

Bring a large pot of water to a gentle boil. Gently add ravioli to boiling water, one at a time, about 6 to a batch. Ravioli have finished cooking 2 minutes after they float to the surface of the water.

Use a slotted spoon to remove cooked ravioli from the water, drain well and transfer to serving plates.

Serve warm, dusted with powdered sugar or drizzled with sauce.

Cream Liqueur sauce

We made this with Kahlua, you can use almost any liqueur you like.

Cornstarch	1 Tbsp	15 ml
Granulated sugar	1/4 cup	50 ml
Heavy whipping cream	2/3 cup	150 ml
Liqueur of choice	1/3 cup	75 ml

In a small saucepan, whisk together corn starch and sugar until well combined. Add heavy whipping cream and continue whisking until well combined and smooth.

Bring to a simmer over medium heat, stirring frequently until mixture thickens. Remove from heat, whisk in liqueur. Use warm or cold.

Panna Cotta

Panna cotta is inherently gluten free, very easy to make, tasty, and impressive - but it tends to slip peoples' minds as being an option, when it comes to figuring out a crowd-pleasing, gluten-free dessert to make. So, let me share my recipes with you!

I have 3 base recipes that I use - one for "basic" panna cotta - this is what I use when I'm flavouring them with either extracts or liqueurs. The second is a fruit based one... which is pretty self explanatory! The third recipe is what I use when I'm making any kind of chocolate panna cotta - it works with white, milk, or dark chocolate. Use baking chocolate bars, or chocolate chips - it's very forgiving!

Basic Panna Cotta

Makes 4 servings

Unflavoured gelatin powder	1 ½ tsp	7 ml
Cold water	3 Tbsp	15 ml
Milk	½ cup	125 ml
Heavy cream	1 1/4 cup	300 ml
Sugar	½ cup	125 ml
Sour cream	½ cup	125 ml
Extract of choice	1-2 tsp	5-10 ml

Sprinkle the gelatin over the cold water in a small bowl and let absorb for five minutes.

Combine milk, heavy cream, and sugar in a saucepan. Heat to just to a simmer, stirring occasionally - do not let it come to boil! Meanwhile, microwave the gelatin for about 15 seconds, or until it's melted.

Once the milk mixture has come to a simmer, remove it from the heat. Whisk in the gelatin until fully incorporated, and the mixture is smooth. Add sour cream and extract, whisking once again till fully incorporated and smooth. Pour into four greased ramekins or custard cups. Chill for at least 2 hours until set.

Serve as-is, or gently unmold onto a serving plate: Dip ramekins or custard cups into hot water for about 10 seconds, wipe dry, and then invert onto plate. If the panna cotta does not dislodge, gently run a knife around the inner edge of the dish and invert.

Variation: Almost any liqueur will work with this recipe - just substitute it for 1/4-1/2 cup of the heavy cream.

Chocolate Panna Cotta

Unflavoured gelatin powder	1 ½ tsp	7 ml
Cold water	3 Tbsp	15 ml
Heavy cream	1 3/4 cup	425 ml
Sugar	½ cup	125 ml
Chocolate of choice, chopped	4 oz	125 g
Sour Cream	½ cup	125 ml
Vanilla extract	1 tsp	5 ml

Sprinkle the gelatin over the cold water in a small bowl and let absorb for five minutes.

Combine heavy cream, and sugar in a saucepan. Heat to just to a simmer, stirring occasionally. Do not let it come to boil! Remove from heat, add chocolate, and stir until chocolate is melted and fully incorporated. Meanwhile, microwave the gelatin for about 15 seconds, or until it's melted.

Whisk the gelatin into the chocolate mixture until fully incorporated, and smooth. Add sour cream, whisking once again till fully incorporated and smooth. Pour into four greased ramekins or custard cups. Chill for at least 2 hours until set.

Serve as-is, or gently unmold onto a serving plate (as described on previous page).

Fruity Panna Cotta

Unflavoured gelatin powder	1 ½ tsp	7 ml
Cold water	3 Tbsp	15 ml
Heavy cream	1 1/4 cup	300 ml
Fruit puree of choice	1 cup	250 ml
Sugar	½ cup	125 ml
Sour Cream	½ cup	125 ml

Sprinkle the gelatin over the cold water in a small bowl and let absorb for five minutes.

Combine heavy cream, fruit puree, and sugar in a saucepan. Heat to just to a simmer, stirring occasionally. Do not let it come to boil! Meanwhile, microwave the gelatin for about 15 seconds, or until it's melted.

Once the cream mixture has come to a simmer, remove it from the heat, and strain through a fine sieve. Whisk in the gelatin until fully incorporated, and the mixture is smooth. Add sour cream, whisking once again till fully incorporated and smooth. Pour into four greased ramekins or custard cups. Chill for at least 2 hours until set.

Serve as-is, or gently unmold onto a serving plate (As described on previous page).

Panna Cotta, Three Ways

173

Truffles

Truffles

My primer on truffles was first published in The Spirited Baker ... but truffles are such a great option for a fancy gluten-free treat, I had to include this here, as a bonus!

Truffles consist of two main parts - the center (chocolate ganache), and the coating. The ganache center is made from just a few very basic ingredients - chocolate, cream, flavouring, and butter. The coating can be made from almost anything - your creativity is pretty much your only limit!

Typically, you'll see store-bought truffles enrobed in chocolate. While that's certainly a popular option, it does veer off into "intimidating" territory - tempering chocolate, etc. Personally, I don't bother - I find rolling truffles in various non-chocolate coatings is not only more fun and less work, I prefer the taste. Tempering chocolate (required for chocolate enrobed truffles) is a bit too involved to get into here - but feel free to use the recipes below for the centers, and research tempering online!

"Stuff to Roll Them In"

- Cocoa powder, coconut flakes, finely chopped nuts, and powdered sugar are all traditional options.. but feel free to go a bit crazy with it. Just be sure that whatever you use is either powdered, or finely chopped.

- Freeze dried fruit is a great option that is readily available for order from online companies. You can pulverize them to a powder for a unique coating!

- Enhance cocoa powder or powdered sugar with the addition of various spices - cinnamon, cardamom, nutmeg, even cayenne pepper... whatever you like. Try using finely powdered dried citrus peels, or a little dried botanicals - rose petals, lavender. Matcha (green tea) powder mixed into powdered sugar is particularly great!

- Fruit powders can be ordered online in various types (see "Resources" section!), and are great to add to cocoa or powdered sugar. Try rolling truffles in exotic powdered fruit such as acai, goji berries, or mangosteen - A little goes a long way! Experiment with amount of flavouring used in your cocoa powder or powdered sugar, have fun with it!

- Finely ground gluten-free cookies of any variety can add an interesting flavour and texture to your truffles. You may want to use store bought cookies for this - their typically-dry texture comes in handy!

- Unique coatings: Try crystallized ginger, maple sugar, crushed coffee beans, finely chopped chocolate, instant hot chocolate powder, crushed pralines, finely crushed gluten-free pretzels, toffee... even potato chips!

As you can see, there are many, many options available for "stuff to roll your truffles in" - and yes, that's a technical term! Mix and match any of these ideas - or anything else you come up with - with the recipes and flavouring options for ganache centers... and the possibilities really are endless!

Chocolate ganache is quite easy to make, but there are a few basic principles to keep in mind:

1. Too much liquid will prevent your ganache from setting up enough to roll properly. Fairly straightforward rule, right? If this happens, try adding extra chocolate... or use your runny ganache as a chocolate fondue or sauce for ice cream!

2. Not all chocolate varieties are created equally. While this applies to flavour, texture, and overall quality, I'm actually talking about behavior. Dark chocolate requires more liquid than milk chocolate, which requires more liquid than white chocolate. Sugar free chocolate requires a smaller amount of liquid than other varieties of chocolate... this is why I have several "basic" recipes here. Please be sure to follow the basic instructions for the variety of chocolate you are using!

3. Water is chocolate's enemy. Be very careful to use a dry bowl, dry utensils, and to not allow any water to fall into your chocolate. Water causes melted chocolate to "seize". Seizing is when melted chocolate comes in contact with even the tiniest amount of water, and becomes grainy, clumpy, and unpleasant. For this reason, you should never use a lid when melting chocolate (condensation will occur, and drip in!), and you should always be careful when using a double boiler.

4. Fat amount is important. The fat content in the chocolate ganache contributes to the smoothness, and the ganache's ability to hold together. Using milk instead of heavy cream really isn't an option. Additionally, if a high percentage of the liquid is coming from a non-fatty source (liqueur, rather than cream), it's a good idea to add extra butter.

5. Liquid added to chocolate must be warm. Pretty basic rule - cold liquid added to melted chocolate will cause it to seize. Warm liquid will not - this is why it's important to heat up the cream mixture before adding it to the chocolate. Do not skip this step!

6. Chocolate chips are just fine to use. Yes, I'm sure the purists just had a heart attack over that phrase... but trust me!

Chocolate chips are an unusual medium for truffle making, consistently being eschewed for bars of pure chocolate. The thing is, however, that not only are chocolate chips are easy to find, they lack the sticker shock that comes with the more traditional chocolate options. I find that this makes chocolate chips a far more accessible option for those who are new to making truffles. Not only that, but they can make a great product, too - only the most avid chocolate connoisseur can really tell the difference between truffles made with a high end bar of chocolate, and those made with a good brand of chocolate chips.

For that reason, I believe chocolate chips are a great way to get in to making truffles. I developed a series of recipes using chocolate chips! Anyone can make these truffles at home, with common ingredients, for only about $4.00/30 truffles. Far less scary of a commitment than the traditional approach!

With all of that said... on to the recipes!

Basic Dark Chocolate Truffles

Good quality dark chocolate chips	12 oz	340 g
Heavy whipping cream	3/4 cup	175 ml
Butter	2 Tbsp	30 ml
Sugar, optional	2 Tbsp	30 ml
Extract of choice	1-2 tsp	5-10 ml
Stuff to roll them in		

Place chocolate chips into a glass mixing bowl, and put aside.

In a small saucepan, combine heavy whipping cream, butter , and sugar. Heat to a boil, remove from heat, stir in extract, if using.

Pour hot cream mixture into bowl of chocolate chips. Let sit for 3-5 minutes. Starting in the middle of the bowl, slowly start stirring the chocolate and cream until all of the chocolate is melted and the cream has disappeared into it – it should be smooth.

Cover with plastic wrap, preferably resting right on top of the surface – this prevents a skin from forming while it cools. Chill in the fridge for at least an hour or two, until it's pretty solid. Once solid, scoop out small amounts (a teaspoon or two), and roll them into balls. Try to handle the chocolate as quickly as possible, or it will melt.

Once all of the ganache is rolled into balls: wash and dry hands, then roll ganache centers in whichever coating(s) you'd like. Store in an airtight container for up to 1 week.

Variation: Substitute a liqueur of choice for 1/4 cup of the heavy whipping cream.

Basic Milk Chocolate Truffles

Good quality milk chocolate chips	10 oz	275 g
Heavy whipping cream	½ cup	125 ml
Butter	2 Tbsp	30 ml
Extract of choice	1-2 tsp	5-10 ml
Stuff to roll them in		

Place chocolate chips into a glass mixing bowl, and put aside.

In a small saucepan, combine heavy whipping cream, and butter. Heat to a boil, remove from heat, stir in extract, if using.

Pour hot cream mixture into bowl of chocolate chips. Let sit for 3-5 minutes. Starting in the middle of the bowl, slowly start stirring the chocolate and cream until all of the chocolate is melted and the cream has disappeared into it – it should be smooth.

Cover with plastic wrap, preferably resting right on top of the surface – this prevents a skin from forming while it cools. Chill in the fridge for at least an hour or two, until it's pretty solid. Once solid, scoop out small amounts (a teaspoon or two), and roll them into balls. Try to handle the chocolate as quickly as possible, or it will melt.

Once all of the ganache is rolled into balls: wash and dry hands, then roll ganache centers in whichever coating(s) you'd like. Store in an airtight container for up to 1 week.

Variation: Substitute a liqueur of choice for 1/4 cup of the heavy whipping cream.

Basic White Chocolate Truffles

Good quality white chocolate chips	12 oz	340 g
Heavy whipping cream	1/3 cup	75 ml
Butter	2 Tbsp	30 ml
Extract of choice	1-2 tsp	5-10 ml
Stuff to roll them in		

Place chocolate chips into a glass mixing bowl, and put aside.

In a small saucepan, combine heavy whipping cream, and butter. Heat to a boil, remove from heat, stir in extract, if using.

Pour hot cream mixture into bowl of chocolate chips. Let sit for 3-5 minutes. Starting in the middle of the bowl, slowly start stirring the chocolate and cream until all of the chocolate is melted and the cream has disappeared into it – it should be smooth.

Cover with plastic wrap, preferably resting right on top of the surface – this prevents a skin from forming while it cools. Chill in the fridge for at least an hour or two, until it's pretty solid. Once solid, scoop out small amounts (a teaspoon or two), and roll them into balls. Try to handle the chocolate as quickly as possible, or it will melt.

Once all of the ganache is rolled into balls: wash and dry hands, then roll ganache centers in whichever coating(s) you'd like. Store in an airtight container for up to 1 week.

Variation: Substitute a liqueur of choice for half of the heavy whipping cream.

Basic Sugar Free Chocolate Truffles

Hershey's Sugar Free chips *	8 oz	225 g
Heavy whipping cream	1/3 cup	75 ml
Butter	2 Tbsp	30 ml
Extract of choice	1-2 tsp	5-10 ml
Stuff to roll them in		

Place chocolate chips into a glass mixing bowl, and put aside.

In a small saucepan, combine heavy whipping cream, and butter. Heat to a boil, remove from heat, stir in extract, if using.

Pour hot cream mixture into bowl of chocolate chips. Let sit for 3-5 minutes. Starting in the middle of the bowl, slowly start stirring the chocolate and cream until all of the chocolate is melted and the cream has disappeared into it – it should be smooth.

Cover with plastic wrap, preferably resting right on top of the surface – this prevents a skin from forming while it cools. Chill in the fridge for at least an hour or two, until it's pretty solid. Once solid, scoop out small amounts (a teaspoon or two), and roll them into balls. Try to handle the chocolate as quickly as possible, or it will melt.

Once all of the ganache is rolled into balls: wash and dry hands, then roll ganache centers in whichever coating(s) you'd like. Store in an airtight container for up to 1 week

* Hershey's is the only brand I've experimented with. Chocolate is finicky, and due to formulation, I'd have to assume that sugar free chocolate is even more so. Go ahead and try this with other brands of sugar free chocolate, but you may find that you need more or less cream. If your ganache doesn't firm up, you have a great chocolate sauce! If it's too firm, remelt it and add a little warm cream to it.

Final carb count on these truffles will depend a lot on what you roll them in, nuts are a great option!

Variation: Substitute a liqueur of choice for 1/4 cup of the heavy whipping cream.

Conversions

To accommodate bakers in different countries and from different cultures, measurements throughout this book have been provided in both U.S. conventional and metric. To keep things simple, measurement conversions have been rounded. See below for the exact conversions, as well as the rounded versions provided throughout this book.

Spoons	Actual Conversion*	Standard Metric Used
1/4 tsp	1.2 ml	1 ml
½ tsp	2.5 ml	2 ml
1 tsp	4.9 ml	5 ml
1 Tbsp	14.8 ml	15 ml

Cups	Actual Conversion*	Standard Metric Used
1/4 cup	59.1 ml	50 ml
1/3 cup	78.9 ml	75 ml
½ cup	118.3 ml	125 ml
2/3 cup	157.7 ml	150 ml
3/4 cup	177.4 ml	175 ml
1 cup	236.6 ml	250 ml
4 cups	946.4 ml	1000 ml / 1 liter

Ounces (Weight)	Actual Conversion*	Standard Metric Used
1 oz	28.3 grams	30 grams
2 oz	56.7 grams	55 grams
3 oz	85.0 grams	85 grams
4 oz	113.4 grams	125 grams
5 oz	141.7 grams	140 grams
6 oz	170.1 grams	170 grams
7 oz	198.4 grams	200 grams
8 oz	226.8 grams	250 grams
16 oz / 1 lb	453.6 grams	500 grams
32 oz / 2 lbs	907.2 grams	1000 grams / 1 kilogram

* Source: Google Calculator

Resources

This list is for informational purposes only, and does not necessarily constitute an endorsement of any of these companies. We do not receive payment of any kind by these companies for being listed here. It is the readers' responsibility to properly vet any companies they choose to do business with; we are not responsible for any disputes that may arise.

Ingredients

Nuts Online
www.nutsonline.com
Gluten-free flours, nuts, dried fruits, fruit powders, and more.

Amazon
www.amazon.com
Gluten-free flours, freeze dried corn

Equipment

Amazon
www.amazon.com
Canoli molds, potato ricer, spaetzel maker, cracker / cookie cutters

Other

Celebration Generation
www.celebrationgeneration.com
Food & lifestyle blog, recipes, photos, and inspiration

Index

Marie Porter

Marie Porter is an Aspergian polymath, which is just a fancy way of saying that she knows a lot of stuff - and does even more stuff - with a brain that runs on a different operating system than most. Because of that OS, her career has spanned across many facets: She's a trained mixologist, competitive cake artist, professional costumer, and - last but not least - author. As of 2016, her written works include 6 cookbooks, 6 specialty sewing manuals, and a tornado memoir. Her work has graced magazines and blogs around the world, she has costumed for Olympians and professional wrestlers, has baked for brides, celebrities, and even Klingons. Marie is now proud to share her wealth of multi-disciplinary knowledge and experience with cooks and seamstresses around the world.

Michael Porter

Michael Porter works in medical manufacturing, and is a food and commercial photographer. His work has appeared in local, national, and international magazines, in catalogs, corporate websites, and as well as in many online media outlets. In addition to being an awesome husband and photographer, Michael is Celebration Generation's "Chief Engineering Officer", responsible for all custom builds, equipment repairs, and warp engine emergencies. After their home was smashed by a tornado, Michael singlehandedly built all of the cabinetry in their new kitchen! In his 'spare' time, Michael is an avid home brewer, and is pursuing a degree in engineering".

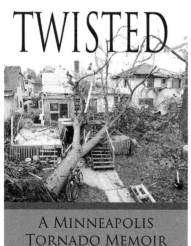

MARIE PORTER

TWISTED

A MINNEAPOLIS TORNADO MEMOIR

Twisted: A Minneapolis Tornado Memoir

On the afternoon of May 22, 2011, North Minneapolis was devastated by a tornado. Twisted recounts the Porters' first 11 months, post tornado. Rebuilding their house, working around the challenges presented by inadequate insurance coverage. Frustration at repeated bouts of incompetence and greed from their city officials. Dealing with issues such as loss of control, logistics, change, and over-stimulation, as two adults with Aspergers. With the help of social media – and the incredibly generous support of the geek community – the Porters were able to emerge from the recovery marathon without too much of a hit to their sanity levels. New friends were made, new skills learned, and a "new" house emerged from the destruction. Twisted is a roller coaster of emotion, personal observations, rants, humor, social commentary, set backs and triumphs. Oh, and details on how to cook jambalaya for almost 300 people, in the parking lot of a funeral home… should you ever find yourself in the position to do so!

The Spirited Baker
Intoxicating Desserts & Potent Potables

Combining liqueurs with more traditional baking ingredients can yield spectacular results. Try Mango Mojito Upside Down Cake, Candy Apple Flan, Jalapeno Beer Peanut Brittle, Lynchburg Lemonade Cupcakes, Pina Colada Rum Cake, Strawberry Daiquiri Chiffon Pie, and so much more.

To further add to your creative possibilities, the first chapter teaches how to infuse spirits to make both basic & cream liqueurs, as well as home made flavor extracts! This book contains over 160 easy to make recipes, with variation suggestions to help create hundreds more!

Evil Cake Overlord
Ridiculously Delicious Cakes

Marie Porter has been known for her "ridiculously delicious" moist cakes and tasty, unique flavors since the genesis of her custom cake business. Now, you can have recipes for all of the amazing flavors on her former custom cake menu, as well as many more! Once you have baked your moist work of gastronomic art, fill & frost your cake with any number of tasty possibilities. Milk chocolate cardamom pear, mango mojito.. even our famous Chai cake – the flavor that got us into "Every Day with Rachel Ray" magazine! Feeling creative? Use our easy to follow recipe to make our yummy fondant. Forget everything you've heard about fondant – ours is made from marshmallows and powdered sugar, and is essentially candy – you can even flavor it to bring a whole new level of "yum!" to every cake you make!

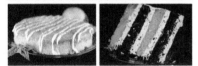

Beyond Flour
A Fresh Approach to Gluten-Free Cooking & Baking

Most gf recipes are developed by taking a "normal" recipe, swapping in a simulated "all purpose" gluten-free flour... whether store bought, or a homemade version. "Beyond Flour" takes a bit of a different approach: developing the recipe from scratch. Rather than just swapping out the flour for an "all purpose" mix, Marie Porter uses various alternative flours as individual ingredients – skillfully blending flavours, textures, and other properties unique to each flour – not making use of any kind of all-purpose flour mix. Supporting ingredients and different techniques are also utilized to achieve the perfect end goal ... not just a "reasonable facsimile". With Beyond Flour, you can now indulge in some of your deepest, darkest guilty pleasure food cravings -safely and joyously!

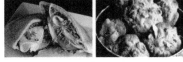

Hedonistic Hops
The HopHead's Guide to Kitchen Badassery

While hops may seem like a bizarre or exotic item to cook with, they're really not that different from any other herb or spice in your cupboard… you just have to know what to do with them! From condiments, sides, & main dishes, to beverages and desserts, Marie Porter creates delicious recipes utilizing hops of various flavour profiles - playing up their unique characteristics - to create recipes full of complex flavour. Much like salt or lemon juice can be added to dishes to perk them up, a small amount of hops - used wisely, and with specific techniques to do so in a balanced fashion - can really make a dish sing. Even those who are not fans of beer will love the unique flavours that various types of hops can bring to their plate. Floral, earthy, peppery, citrusy… Cooking with hops is a great way to expand your seasoning arsenal!

Beyond Flour 2
A Fresh Approach to Gluten-Free Cooking & Baking

How many times have you come across a gluten-free recipe claiming to be "just as good as the normal version!", only to find that the author must have had some skewed memories on what the "normal" version tasted, looked, and/or felt like? How many times have you felt the need to settle for food with weird after-taste, gummy consistency, or cardboard-like texture, convinced that this is your new lot in life?

Continuing where its predecessor left off, "Beyond Flour 2"is full of tasty gluten-free recipes that have been developed from scratch to be the absolute best they can be - as good or better than the "real" thing - with no "all purpose" mixes, and no need to compromise on taste or texture!

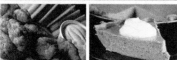

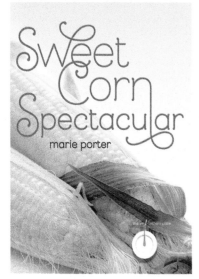

Sweet Corn Spectacular
(Minnesota Historical Society Press)

The height of summer brings with it the bounty of fresh sweet corn Grilled or boiled, slathered in butter and sprinkled with salt, corn on the cob is a mainstay of cook-out menus. But this "vegetable" can grace your plate in so many other ways. In fact, author and baker Marie Porter once devised an entire day's worth of corn-based dishes to celebrate her "corn freak"husband's birthday. "Sweet Corn Spectacular" displays Porter's creative and flavor-filled approach to this North American original, inspiring year-round use of this versatile ingredient and tasty experimenting in your own kitchen. As Porter reminds home cooks, the possibilities are endless!

Introducing Marie Porter's "Spandex Simplified" Series

Prior to her recipe development career, Marie Porter had an illustrious career in spandex costuming. Now, you can learn all of her secrets to spandex design and sewing!

"Synchro Swimwear", "Sewing for Skaters", "Sewing for Gymnasts", "Fitness & Bodybuilding", "Sewing for Superheroes", and "Custom Swimwear" are the first six titles in Marie's Spandex Simplified series, and are all about designing and creating spectacular and durable competitive and recreational sports apparel and costuming. "Sewing for Dancers" is scheduled for a 2017 release.

These books are appropriate for beginner to advanced levels of sewing ability, and are written from both a designer, and former "performance" athlete's point of view. They teach everything from the basics, to tricks of the trade. The "Spandex Simplified" series will prepare the reader to design and make almost any design of competitive synchro suit, skating dress, gymnastics leotard, posing suit, swimsuit, or spandex cosplay imaginable.

Given the cost of decent custom spandex garments, these manuals each pay for themselves with the savings from just one project!

The books are written completely in laymans' terms and carefully explained, step by step. Only basic sewing knowledge and talent is required. Learn everything from measuring and pattern alteration, to easily creating ornate applique designs, and embellishing the finished suit in one book!

For complete Tables of Contents, more info, and to order, visit

www.spandexsimplified.com

To order any or all of Celebration Generation's titles, visit us online at

www.celebrationgeneration.com

CPSIA information can be obtained
at www.ICGtesting.com
Printed in the USA
LVOW05s1524151016

508683LV00005B/5/P

9 780997 660821